New Directions for
Student Services

Elizabeth J. Whitt
EDITOR-IN-CHIEF

John H. Schuh
ASSOCIATE EDITOR

Advancing the Integrity of Professional Practice

Robert B. Young

EDITOR

Number 135 • Fall 2011
Jossey-Bass
San Francisco

ADVANCING THE INTEGRITY OF PROFESSIONAL PRACTICE
Robert B. Young (ed.)
New Directions for Student Services, no. 135
Elizabeth J. Whitt, Editor-in-Chief
John H. Schuh, Associate Editor

NEW DIRECTIONS FOR STUDENT SERVICES (ISSN 0164-7970, e-ISSN 1536-0695) is part of The Jossey-Bass Higher and Adult Education Series and is published quarterly by Wiley Subscription Services, Inc., A Wiley Company, at Jossey-Bass, 989 Market Street, San Francisco, California 94103-1741. Periodicals Postage Paid at San Francisco, California, and at additional mailing offices. POSTMASTER: Send address changes to New Directions for Student Services, Jossey-Bass, 989 Market Street, San Francisco, CA 94103-1741.

New Directions for Student Services is indexed in CIJE: Current Index to Journals in Education (ERIC), Contents Pages in Education (T&F), Current Abstracts (EBSCO), Education Index/Abstracts (H.W. Wilson), Educational Research Abstracts Online (T&F), ERIC Database (Education Resources Information Center), and Higher Education Abstracts (Claremont Graduate University).

Microfilm copies of issues and articles are available in 16mm and 35mm, as well as microfiche in 105mm, through University Microfilms Inc., 300 North Zeeb Road, Ann Arbor, Michigan 48106-1346.

SUBSCRIPTIONS cost $89.00 for individuals and $259.00 for institutions, agencies, and libraries in the United States.

EDITORIAL CORRESPONDENCE should be sent to the Editor-in-Chief, Elizabeth J. Whitt, N473 Lindquist Center, The University of Iowa, Iowa City, IA 52242.

www.josseybass.com

CONTENTS

EDITOR'S NOTES   1
Robert B. Young

1. The Virtues of Organizational Integrity   5
Robert B. Young
Divisions of student affairs must be structurally sound and orient their
efforts to promote ethical change to the characteristics of different
types of colleges and universities.

2. Integrity in Student Affairs Organizations   15
Leonard Baird
Student affairs needs to create an environment in which students, staff,
and administrators are accountable for their actions and policies, in
order to deal with changing demands from stakeholders.

3. Promoting Integrity through Standards of Practice   27
Susan R. Komives and Jan Arminio
The Council for the Advancement of Standards can help administrators understand, assess, and maintain the integrity of student affairs
functions for accreditation and internal improvement.

4. Integrity in Transactional Leadership   35
Thomas Miller
Student affairs administrators need to conduct their transactions with
students in clear, consistent, honest, and open ways to maintain
integrity.

5. Transformational Leadership, Integrity, and Power   45
Laura M. Harrison
Transformational leadership is a valuable ideal, but student affairs
administrators need to know how to negotiate complex political realities if they want to build institutional integrity.

6. Integrity in Student Development   53
Dennis C. Roberts and Trudy W. Banta
The authors engage in a dialogue about theory and practice, and
promote assessment as a means to improve the integrity of student
development.

7. Teaching Integrity   67
Sue Saunders and Jennifer Lease Butts
Integrity can be an important element in professional preparation
programs and in continuing professional education.

8. Give In or Get Out? Responding to Professional Challenges   79
Robert B. Young
The author presents themes from interviews with several student
affairs administrators about challenges to their integrity.

9. Gone With the Wind? Integrity and Hurricane Katrina   89
Frances Lucas and Brit Katz
The past president and vice president of student affairs describe how
they tried to maintain the integrity of Millsaps College in the aftermath
of Hurricane Katrina.

INDEX   97

EDITOR'S NOTES

> The academy must lead with integrity in order to serve society, not to be
> saved by society. This is not just its legal requirement; it is its moral opportu-
> nity, and thus its essential obligation (Young, 1997).

Those words were an echo as much as a shout when I wrote them 14
years ago. In 1902, one of the forebears of student affairs practice, Le Baron
Russell Briggs, wrote that "a college must be an institution of truth; as a
school of character, it must be a school of integrity. It can have no other
justification" (p. 66).

Briggs would be surprised by most of the challenges that confront
higher education today, and relieved that integrity is still essential to their
resolution. A century after Briggs's remarks, the Middle States Association
[MSA] declared: "Integrity is a central, indispensable and defining hallmark
of effective higher education institutions" (MSA, 2002, p. 18). The MSA
requires colleges and universities to demonstrate integrity in order to be
accredited within its region of service.

No one is going to argue with the requirement to have integrity. It is
pasted onto the names of every type of business enterprise, because the
term inspires the same good feelings as *community,* another word "that virtually no one has taken the trouble to quarrel with; even its worst enemies
praise it" (Berry, 1987, p. 179). Enron put integrity on company paper-
weights and bragged: "When we say we will do something, we will do it;
when we say we cannot or will not do something, then we won't do it."
Even its worst enemies praise integrity.

At least Enron defined what it meant by integrity. Most organizations
do not, because everyone "thinks they know what integrity is" (Badaracco
& Ellsworth, 1989, p. 96). So what if one author called it a virtue that cannot be specified (MacIntyre, 1987) and others confuse integrity with other
concepts (Becker, 1998)? Why worry about that? Why puzzle over a sooth-
ing concept that everyone believes they understand?

The authors and I did not puzzle over a definition of integrity before
we started to write. We steered our first efforts on our own assumptions.
After I received the first few chapters, I induced this definition of integrity
from what had been written: integrity is the combination of attributes and
actions that makes people and organizations coherent, consistent, and
potentially ethical. Some of the authors worked with this definition when
they refined their chapters for publication.

The chapters illustrate how student affairs administrators can understand and implement integrity in their institutions. Some chapters are conceptual, most mix concepts with practice, and one chapter is carved from a
tragic event. Integrity is not just a proclamation in mission statements; nor

is it just a component of leadership training. Integrity is, as well, a test offered at any hour. Passing it is seldom rewarded, but failing it can ruin lives. Student affairs administrators must know what integrity requires in all its forms if they want to protect and expand the worth of higher education. Goodwill and benign intentions will not do that job (Paine, 1997); the integrity of student affairs requires abundant reflection, deliberate planning, hard choices, and even harder work.

Organizational Perspectives

The first three chapters concern the organizational integrity of student affairs. Lynn Paine (1997) wrote that organizational integrity requires self-governance, responsibility, moral soundness, adherence to principle, and constancy of purpose. This list, like others (e.g., Becker, 1998), promotes two major attributes, structural soundness and ethical direction. In the first chapter, I explore these attributes and relate them to archetypes of colleges and universities. Then I offer some comments about the structural and ethical integrity of student affairs practice.

Paine (1997) added that employees with integrity are "committed to the organization's purposes and ideals" (p. 98). But what happens when institutional priorities work against the purposes and ideals of a unit such as student affairs? In the second chapter, Leonard Baird asks readers to reaffirm their central commitment to student welfare, and create an environment that holds students, staff, and administrators accountable for their efforts, despite external pressures.

The Council for the Advancement of Standards [CAS] was established to support the assessment of student affairs operations. In the third chapter, two CAS presidents, Susan Komives and Jan Arminio, examine the role, requirements, recommendations, and success of the Council in regard to the integrity of student affairs functions.

Leadership Perspectives

Transactional and transformational leadership perspectives are discussed in the second section of this issue. Stephen Carter (1996) declared that integrity means knowing the difference between right and wrong, saying that one intends to do what is right even at personal cost, and doing it. Thus, if leadership means doing the right thing and management means doing things right, then integrity is a synonym for leadership. Integrity is the right thing done (Cohen, 2001).

That notion is easy to appreciate, but it belies the practical work one needs to do, to "do things right." In the fourth chapter, Thomas Miller examines the bottom-line obligations of student affairs administrators in their transactions with students, and in the next chapter, Laura Harrison writes about the practical strategies that are needed to make transformational changes in our institutions.

NEW DIRECTIONS FOR STUDENT SERVICES • DOI: 10.1002/ss

Education and Integrity

The next section of this issue ties education to integrity. In their chapter, Dennis Roberts and Trudy Banta engage in a dialogue about the way student development theory should guide practice, and how its assessment is essential to maintain the integrity of our practice. Sue Saunders and Jennifer Lease Butts consider how we should teach integrity to graduate students and new professionals in Chapter 7.

Integrity in Crisis

The last two chapters are about challenges to integrity. Some are expected, and others surprise us, usually at the worst possible times (Kidder, 1995). Hall directors deal with challenges whenever their residents are celebrating at three o'clock on a Saturday morning. Those challenges are part of their normal work routines, but other, unforeseen circumstances test our purposes, communication, values, and adaptive strategies under fire (Bennis & Thomas, 2002). In Chapter 8, I share what I learned from six student affairs leaders who were pressured to sell out their principles or get out of professional positions. In the final chapter, Frances Lucas and Brit Katz describe how an overwhelming challenge, Hurricane Katrina, affected the integrity of services, staff, and students at Millsaps College.

Conclusion

Readers of this volume will learn how integrity affects the trustworthiness of their organizations and operations. They will have the opportunity to read about the highest goals and the best practices of leadership, and gain ideas about some practical strategies that can help them deal with challenges to organizational and individual integrity.

References

Badaracco, J., and Ellsworth, R. *Leadership and the Quest for Integrity*. Cambridge, MA: Harvard Business School Press, 1989.

Becker, T. "Integrity in Organizations: Beyond Honesty and Conscientiousness." *Academy of Management Review*, 1998, 23(1), 154–162.

Bennis, W., and Thomas, R. "Crucibles of Leadership." *Harvard Business Review*, 2002, 80(9), 7.

Berry, W. *Home Economics: Fourteen Essays*. San Francisco: North Point Press, 1987.

Briggs, L. *School, College, and Character*. Boston: Houghton, Mifflin, and Co., 1902.

Carter, S. "The insufficiency of Honesty." *The Atlantic Monthly*, 1996, 2, 74–76.

Cohen, W. Leading with integrity. *Executive Excellence*, 2001,17.

Kidder, R. *How Good People Make Tough Choices*. New York: William Morrow, 1995.

Macintyre, A. *After Virtue: A Study in Moral Theory*. Notre Dame, IN: University of Notre Dame Press, 1987.

Middle States Association. Characteristics of Excellence in Higher Education: Eligibility requirements and standards for accreditation. Found on May 25, 2002 at http://www.msache.org/pubs.html

Paine, L. *Cases in Leadership, Ethics, and Organizational Integrity*. Chicago: Irwin, 1997.

Young, R. *No Neutral Ground: Standing by the Values We Prize in Higher Education*. San Francisco: Jossey-Bass, 1997.

ROBERT B. YOUNG is a professor of higher education and student affairs (HESA) in the Patton College of Education and Human Services at Ohio University.

NEW DIRECTIONS FOR STUDENT SERVICES • DOI: 10.1002/ss

1

Structural and ethical forms of integrity are described, related to three archetypes of colleges and universities, and connected to the integrity of student affairs practice.

The Virtues of Organizational Integrity

Robert B. Young

In the Editor's Notes, integrity was defined as a combination of attributes and actions that makes individuals and organizations coherent, consistent, and potentially ethical. Several aspects of that definition are emphasized in this chapter. Consistency and coherence are part of the structural integrity of entities. Ethical integrity is the moral force that emanates from sound structures. A church building can have structural integrity and no moral worth, but the congregation inside that building should endorse sound principles as well as a sound roof. To say that another way, structural and ethical integrity reflect planes of ethics, legally standardized at the base and morally compelling on top of that. "Do no harm" is secured at the start, and then the benefits can be taken into account.

At the start of this chapter, I describe the organizational virtues that are associated with structural and ethical integrity. Virtues are the focus instead of behaviors, traits, or values, because virtues contain all these components: the stable characteristics of traits, the behaviors that are evidence of traits, and the values that guide behaviors (Trevino, Hartman, & Brown, 2000). Next, the virtues of structural and ethical integrity are related to collegial, empirical, and political archetypes of higher education institutions. The structural and ethical integrity of student affairs is the topic of the third part of the chapter, and it concludes with some suggestions for organizational analysis and practice.

Structural Integrity

In Chapter 6, Dennis Roberts and Trudy Banta connect integrity to its original meaning of wholeness. MacIntyre (1987) wrote that wholeness is the

New Directions for Student Services, no. 135, Fall 2011 © Wiley Periodicals, Inc.
Published online in Wiley Online Library (wileyonlinelibrary.com) • DOI: 10.1002/ss.399

only specific referent of integrity; in other words, the sum of integrity is not disjointed arms and legs but a coherent body.

Thus, coherence is one of the virtues of structural integrity. Everything fits together. Consistency is the other virtue, and it connotes reliability. While the structural integrity of an object depends on consistent but static materials, the integrity of people and organizations is always in motion. Actions are judged by their consistency with other actions. People become suspicious when a liar or an Enron acts with honor, because this behavior does not mesh with the lifestyle of the individual or the organization (MacIntyre, 1987; Musschenga, 2001).

Ethical Integrity

Organizations with ethical integrity are structurally coherent and consistent, but they are ethically effective as well as functionally efficient. They are self-governing, responsible, morally sound, principled (Paine, 1997), and altruistic instead of egocentric (Musschenga, 2001). Carter (1996) wrote that the virtues of integrity are very laudable when we risk harming ourselves to serve others, and less so when we risk harming others to serve ourselves: "Integrity and self-interest often coincide, but often they do not and it is at those moments that our integrity is truly tested" (p. 75).

The Virtues of Ethical Integrity. Many books about integrity gestate in the same way. Retired CEOs ponder the merits of their careers, and pen books about ethical leadership and organizational integrity. They list the virtues that made them successful, assume that those virtues will bring success to any leader in any organization, and write a chapter about each virtue on their list. A few of these books are wildly successful. Most disappear quickly, and all of them offer a modern medley of the seven "cardinal" virtues that were prized by the Ancients. The Greeks liked four secular ones: courage, temperance, justice, and prudence. The apostle Paul espoused three sacred ones: faith, hope, and love (also known as charity). The latter three are "humble" alternatives to the "heroic" four that predate them (MacIntyre, 1987). They promote cooperation instead of competition. In modern parlance, the humble virtues constitute a new paradigm of leadership—what has been called *Leading with Soul* (Bolman & Deal, 1997)—instead of the old paradigm of individualized, heroic leadership.

Relating the Virtues of Integrity to Different Types of Institutions. In the Editor's Notes, I wrote that integrity has always been important to higher education. The need for it is constantly affirmed, but different notions about integrity are in play in different types of colleges and universities.

American higher education has more than 3,000 institutions but just a handful of archetypes. The three primary ones can be called collegial, empirical, and political, and each of them is associated with different virtues. The collegial archetype emphasizes the humble ethics of a quasi-sacred community of scholars; the empirical one, the structural coherence and consistency that come from scientific logic; and the political archetype, the heroic virtues that are needed to cope with modern chaos.

Many faculty were lured into the academy because they wanted to join an extended family of scholars who debate ideas in a haven away from the chaos of modern society. This is the idealized culture of the liberal arts college. It prizes collaboration, mutual respect, order, and personal sustenance: in other words, the faith, hope, and love that constitute the virtues of caring.

The empirical or bureaucratic institution developed because the collegial one was too small, too subjective, and too slow-paced to deal with an urbanizing world. In the early 1900s, social philosophers contended that scientifically based organizations could deal with larger and more complex issues than organizations that relied on familial relationships for their structure. Scientific laws would create greater consistency, coherence, and tangible successes than natural law ever could.

In 1971, J. Victor Baldridge wrote that the university had grown too large and too diverse to be ruled by either natural or scientific laws. He articulated the importance of the political archetype in which interest groups coalesce and collide, and decisions are made through negotiation. The political archetype is less cordial than the collegial one and less coherent than the empirical one, but it emphasizes important virtues such as prudence, diversity, and the courage to change. These secular virtues can mean as much to organizational integrity as the sacred virtues of caring or the rational virtues of sound structures.

The Organizational Integrity of Student Affairs

Over the past quarter century, researchers have pinned the following values on student affairs practice: self-awareness, independence, tolerance, respect, and fairness (Dalton & Healy, 1984); honesty, fairness, integrity, predictability, courage, and confidentiality (Upcraft, 1988); aesthetics, altruism, community, equality, freedom, human dignity, justice, and truth (Young, 1993); holism, individuality, agency, interaction, context, intentionality, grounded practice, teaching, collaboration, citizenship, and accountability (Evans & Reason, 2001); and honesty, trust, fairness, respect, and responsibility (Baird, Chapter 2). Thus, student affairs practice boasts some heroic virtues (e.g., independence, awareness, agency, fairness, freedom, intentionality), some humble virtues (e.g., community, equality, context, trust, altruism, human dignity, collaboration), and two structural ones (grounded practice, accountability).

The humble virtues of student affairs are a good match for the collegial model of an institution; its heroic virtues fit the political one. The fit brings comfort, but conflict can be equally important. The humble virtues of student affairs can temper the atomistic excesses of the political institution, and the heroic virtues can help differentiate people and situations in the collegial one.

But before any individuals involved in student affairs boast the popularity or potential of their espoused ethical virtues, they should attend to critics who think that student affairs has no structural integrity. These critics might call it a hodgepodge of appendages: a collection of arms and toes and fingers with no apparent connection to the spine, head, or heart of the academy.

The Structural Integrity of Student Affairs

Student affairs has been called many names, served many purposes, and offered many services over the past hundred years, but it has never resolved a conflict between its general philosophy and its specific identity. Today's administrative unit known as student *affairs* can also be called student *services*. Fifty years ago, it was student *personnel* or student *personnel services*. This administrative entity contains an array of student resource functions that seem related, but they are not proprietary. At some institutions, the admissions office is listed under student affairs. At others, it is part of academic affairs, administrative affairs, or a distinct area called enrollment management. Enrollment management is a conception and collection of services that might report to student affairs, the provost, or the president of an institution. Student affairs might also include residential life but not housing, and student activities but not the union. Sometimes an organizational chart shows student *development* and student *service* subsets of a division of student affairs, and this fosters a perception that some student affairs functions are educational and others are not.

Yet everything in student affairs is supposed to be guided by an educational philosophy that is in effect all the time and everywhere. For example, dormitories must be called "residence halls" because educational programming is as important as a good night's sleep. These halls and all the other operations of student affairs share a historical viewpoint that is supported by modern theories of student development and a learner-centered paradigm of practice. But since this viewpoint, its theories, and paradigm are supposed to affect all the educational endeavors of the institution all of the time, they do not fuse any specific functions into a consistent and coherent student affairs structure.

Empirical Consistency and Coherence.   The student personnel point of view was based on a collegial ideal of caring relationships, but when student affairs became a set of administrative functions, caring became a commodity that was contracted to specialists instead of an obligation across the institution. The 1937 *Student Personnel Point of View* (American Council on Education, 1937) was intended to be an empirical explanation of the purposes and functions of student affairs, but the authors did not: (1) deconstruct the general philosophy of the field in order to identify the exclusive philosophical purview of student affairs, (2) designate and focus the specific functions within that philosophical domain, and (3) eschew all other services and functions outside this realm of philosophy and practice. That would have been the empirical way to establish a new specialization.

Empiricism celebrates the development of sound structures that are conceptually organized, fulfill specific purposes, and are continually assessed. Its scientific approach to organizations and management is allegedly fairer, more consistent, and more coherent than the informal, traditional approach in the collegial culture, because the assumptions of the institution are made evident and tested, and the rules are applied to all of the members and functions of the academy.

Many student affairs professionals recognize the importance of empirical devices like strategic planning, data-informed decision-making, and research activities (e.g., Barr & Sandeen, 2006; Woodard, Love, & Komives, 2000). In Chapter 4, Thomas Miller touts the integrity of clear and consistent operations, and Trudy Banta calls for empirical accountability in Chapter 6. Still, many practitioners seem to think that empirical ideas and instruments represent a left-brained, White male, European, justice-based paradigm of low-order, transactional administration instead of a new rainbow-hued, multiethnic, caring-based paradigm of high-order, transformational leadership (Woodard et al., 2000). Three things might be considered before committing to this viewpoint: (1) empiricism represents the virtues of consistency and coherence to a majority of academics and administrators; (2) empiricism provides a base for prudent and fair decision making, which is required in organizations with ethical integrity; and (3) by disparaging empiricism, student affairs professionals create perceptions that they are too self-absorbed or just incapable of using logic to support their structures and decisions.

The critics of higher education look for empirical data to support the worth of any entity within it, and some indict student affairs as an inconsistent array of incoherent functions with professional pretentions (Penney, 1969, for one). Few, if any, of these critics would argue that ethical integrity could be built on a morally exclusive foundation, and arguing the virtue of empirical flimsiness is self-defeating. It results in what Charles Schroeder (Thomas, 2002) decried as "the all too common self-flagellating, Rodney Dangerfield attitude, 'we don't get no respect.' This all too common attitude has bothered me for decades and yet I have found solace in Elizabeth Blake's assertion that 'the best solution is not to claim professional standing but to show it" (p. 67). Schroeder added, "The most important response is simply this—tie what you do to what matters most in your institution" (p. 67). Empirical credibility is academe's secular equivalent of the rock on which any sacred church is supposed to be founded.

Ethical Integrity and Student Affairs.   Some administrators might argue that it is impossible to measure the true value of many student affairs programs through traditional, empirical measures. Institution-wide caring is educationally profound but statistically immeasurable, and serving underrepresented student groups is morally important even though it is politically disadvantaged by the numbers of members in those groups and the amount of power of entrenched interests. True enough: empirical measures can become overly important, and used to frustrate student affairs units that are overt about making an institution more ethically coherent and the students within it, more ethically whole individuals. When that happens, the fault might not lie with the measures, *per se*, as much as with the respective skills of the people who use them.

Ethical Ideals.   Political institutions show pictures of faculty, students, and trees on every web site and in every view book, in order to delude applicants that these are communal places instead of atomistic enterprises. Many potential students want to believe that they can find the humble virtues of faith, hope, and love on campus, the virtues that hold a community together. Faith is what we believe that we cannot prove to be true; hope is the emotion that faith inspires (Terkel, 2003), and love is the behavior that comes through hope (Atwood, 2003), even when it is euphemized as collegiality or collaboration or community. In many institutions, student affairs programs and functions offer the only semblance of these humble virtues, and the collegial climate, that students will find when they get to campus.

Supposedly, "everybody knows your name" in a collegial institution, and, in some of them, everybody questions whatever you do that is outside institutional norms. In some small religious institutions, conformity connects a student (or an administrative unit) to the singular Truth of God and saves both from the sins of secular individualism (Young, 2001). In collegial institutions with homogeneous students, faculty, programs, and purposes, student affairs units would have an ethical responsibility to free individuality however they can.

Compromising Realities.   Few agencies are charged with promoting communal education in large universities (Boyer, 1990), emancipating individuality in small colleges, and staying attuned to the cultures of both institutions. Fulfilling that charge requires equal devotion to humble and heroic virtues. Many times, the noble process and purpose of this attention are corrupted: caring is contracted to the highest bidders, and conformity becomes the primary goal.

Contractual Caring.   Student affairs specialists care about students, and in many institutions the specific nature of affection is defined by empirical contracts more than communal covenants. A covenant represents the past, present, and future relationships of an entire culture, while a contract is an ephemeral agreement to exchange one thing for another (Westhues, 2004). In political institutions, powerful individuals and temporary coalitions weigh the costs and benefits of caring, determine how much of it should be provided to whom (McCloskey, 1993), and bless the recipients with increased status and attention.

McIntyre (1987) complained that the political culture is unfit to act as moral educator of any community because it engages in activities like contractual caring. Ethical caring is not based in egoism, or negotiated for particular political purposes. The humble virtues are meant to connect, lift, and integrate people beyond their differences, a purpose that might be as noble as ending disenfranchisement or as mundane as getting admissions officers to talk with financial aid officers. Ethical caring is inherently holistic and coherent, and it is rare in political cultures, even among student affairs professionals. The reality is that status becomes more important than synergy for causes, functions, and people. In popular parlance, "It's a [fill in the blank] thing, you won't understand," until my status is cared for more than yours. Thus, until you prove that you love me more, I will not love you more. That type of contract originates in faithlessness, is devoid of hope, and promises only nine-to-five love.

Contractual Conformity. The contractual process can be used to squelch individual development. In institutions large and small, student affairs practitioners are supposed to keep the dogs off campus, the students on, and the atmosphere free of discontent. New recreation centers and student unions are built to woo new students, to absorb the energy of current ones, and to maintain campus stability. If it all works, everyone seems content. Students do not complain, parents pay tuition and fees, alumni donate funds, and legislators do not slash and burn the budget.

The perpetrators of these politics are institutional cheerleaders who are conditioned to conform. Many student affairs administrators were student senators, admissions guides, or resident assistants. Some learned how to get along as undergraduates and now, how to go along with presidents. Their leadership means are compromise or consensus, and their goal, the absence of conflict. They hire people like themselves, and, whenever possible, they hire graduates of the home institution. That phenomenon might be especially true in small colleges, but it is welcomed in political institutions if not respected, because any loyalty contrasts with the chaos of the institution at large. Either way: conformity is not community, and in-breeding does not cultivate genetic success.

Suggestions for Practice

It is easy to ask student affairs divisions and staff to provide courageous alternatives to conformity, but it is unethical to demand alternatives that could never work. The heroic virtues boost the development of individuals, but they also include the virtues of temperance, prudence, and justice. They do not support foolishness. Temperance means that an organization is neither self-indulgent nor self-negating; prudence means that it makes the best choices *possible*; and justice means that it is fair to one and all. Without those other virtues, individual or organizational courage is not heroic; it is reckless derring-do.

With that caveat in mind, the following are recommended for organizational analysis and practice:

- Compare what the division of student affairs thinks is essential to the virtues that other groups prize at the institution.
- Focus on areas where virtues converge or clash, and balance priorities in areas in which challenges are needed and supports can be given.
- Recognize that those groups will view any attempt to change an institution as a violation of its integrity unless there is a balance of challenge and support.
- Examine the organizational structure of the division in comparison to related functional units, and work to make it as organizationally coherent within the institution as possible.
- Closely align goals with structures for the same reason.
- Make consistent, empirical assessments of the impact of the division on retention, growth, satisfaction, involvement, and postgraduation support of the institution.
- Utilize these data to support changes on behalf of underrepresented groups in small, relatively homogeneous institutions.
- Utilize them to reinforce a pervasive, collegial role of student affairs in large, heterogeneous institutions.

Conclusion

Integrity has two different dimensions, structural and ethical. Ethical integrity has its own dimensions, humble and heroic, which are, respectively, communal and individualistic. In psychology, the humble and heroic virtues represent integration and differentiation. Both must cohere to make a healthy person (Sanford, 1980) or, in this discussion, an organization with integrity.

An organization with integrity avoids the excesses of differentiation that tear the whole apart and, at the same time, reduces the excesses of integration that prevent it from being unique. The leader with integrity understands what the overall organization needs for this to happen, and moves his or her unit to counter the excesses that turn virtues into vice. In a collegial culture, courage, temperance, prudence, and justice relieve claustrophobic conformity. In the political environment, the humble virtues of universal love, faith, and hope counter excessive differentiation. The goal is wholeness and the leader's approach is balanced ethical dissonance, what learning theorists might call plus-one challenge and support.

Until the structural integrity of student affairs is reinforced, its attempts at ethical reform might be viewed as self-absorbed dalliance. In this chapter and throughout this volume, empirical means are touted because they demonstrate the consistency and coherence of student affairs to skeptics outside our field. These means are not ends in themselves; they are methods that remind us to declare, design, implement, and evaluate our operations, so that we can be credible forces in advancing the ethical integrity of our institutions.

References

American Council on Education. "The Student Personnel Point of View (1937)." Reprinted in G. Saddlemire and A. Rentz (eds.), *Student Affairs: A Profession's Heritage.* Alexandria, VA: American College Personnel Association, 1986.

Atwood, M. "Hope Springs Eternal." *The New York Review,* 2003, November 6, 78-80. Retrieved on January 12, 2011 at http://www.nybooks.com/articles/archives/2003/nov/06/he-springs-eternal/

Baldridge, J. V. *Power and Conflict in the University: Research in the Sociology of Complex Organizations.* New York: John Wiley, 1971.

Barr, M., and Sandeen, A. *Critical Issues for Student Affairs: Challenges and Opportunities.* San Francisco: John Wiley, 2006.

Bolman, L., and Deal, T. *Leading with Soul.* San Francisco: Jossey-Bass, 1997.

Boyer, E. *Campus Life: In Search of Community.* Princeton, N.J.: The Carnegie Foundation for the Advancement of Teaching, 1990.

Carter, S. "The Insufficiency of Honesty." *The Atlantic Monthly,* 1996, 2, 74–76.

Dalton, J., and Healy, M. "Using Values Education Activities to Confront Student Conduct Issues." *NASPA Journal,* 1984, 22, 19–25.

Evans, N., and Reason, R. "Guiding Principles: A Review and Analysis of Student Affairs Philosophical Statements." *Journal of College Student Development,* 2001, 42, 3–37.

McCloskey, D. "Bourgeois Blues." *Reason,* 1993, 5. Retrieved January 5, 2007 from http://reason.com/9305/mccloskey.shtml

MacIntyre, A. *After Virtue: A Study in Moral Theory.* Notre Dame, IN: University of Notre Dame Press, 1987.

Musschenga, A. "Education for Moral Integrity." *Journal of Philosophy of Education,* 2001, 35(2), 219–235.

Paine, L. *Cases in Leadership, Ethics, and Organizational Integrity.* Chicago: Irwin, 1997.

Penney, J. "Student Personnel Work: A Profession Stillborn." *Personnel and Guidance Journal,* 1969, 47, 958-962.

Sanford, N. *Learning after College.* Orinda, CA: Montaigne, 1980.

Terkel, S. *Hope Dies Last: Keeping the Faith in Difficult Times.* New York: New Press, 2003.

Thomas,W. "Moral Domain of Student Affairs Leadership." In J. Dalton and M. McClinton (eds.), *The Art and Practical Wisdom of Student Affairs Leadership.* New Directions for Student Services, no. 98. San Francisco: Jossey Bass, 2002.

Trevino, L., Hartman, L., and Brown, M. "Moral Person and Moral Manager: How Executives Develop a Reputation for Ethical Leadership." *California Management Review,* 2000, 42(4), 128–43.

Upcraft, M. "Managing Right." In M. Upcraft and M. Barr (eds.), *Managing Student Affairs Effectively.* New Directions for Student Services, 1988, 42. San Francisco: Jossey-Bass.

Westhues, K. *The Trial, Degradation, and Dismissal of a Professor: Administrative Mobbing in Academe.* Lewiston, NY: Edwin Mellen Press, 2004.

Woodard, D., Love, P., and Komives, S. *Leadership and Management Issues for a New Century.* New Directions in Student Services, 2000, 92. San Francisco: Jossey-Bass.

Young, R. "Essential Values of the Profession." In R. Young (ed.), *Identifying and Implementing the Essential Values of the Profession*. New Directions in Student Services, 1993, *61*. San Francisco: Jossey-Bass, 5–14.

Young, R. "Colleges on the Crossroads." *Current Issues in Catholic Higher Education*, 2001, 65–82.

ROBERT B. YOUNG *is a professor of higher education and student affairs (HESA) in the Patton College of Education and Human Services at Ohio University.*

NEW DIRECTIONS FOR STUDENT SERVICES • DOI: 10.1002/ss

2

Student affairs administrators need to create an environment that protects student welfare, and they need to develop the skills to deal with external and internal challenges to the integrity of higher education.

Integrity in Student Affairs Organizations

Leonard Baird

Integrity is a term that is intuitively appealing, but hard to define and implement. This chapter discusses those conceptual complexities as well as an ideal portrait of organizations with integrity, a description of the challenges to the integrity of organizations, a discussion of the enhancement of integrity through compliance programs and changes in the culture, and the implications for the preparation of graduate students.

A Philosophical Description

Let us begin with a philosophical view and consider how integrity concerns consistency among the parts of the self, behaving morally, and is usually applied to individuals. At the individual level, integrity involves the integration of the self, maintenance of identity, standing for something, moral purpose, and virtue (Cox, LaCaze, & Levine, 2008). How do these aspects of integrity apply to organizations, such as divisions of student affairs? The organizational feature corresponding to the integration of the self is the extent to which the organization has a clear, consistent set of purposes and practices that guide its activities. Thus, the mission statement should be internally consistent, and the activities of the organization need to reflect these aspirations. The purposes and practices should be lasting ones, not easily changed by the whims of events, and they should be ones the organization's members can adopt wholeheartedly (Cox, LaCaze, & Levine, 2008).

The identity aspect of integrity involves acting in a way that accurately reflects your sense of who you are, acting with motives and commitments that are most deeply your own (Williams, 1981). Organizationally, this requires serious discussions of the essential values of the unit and the

NEW DIRECTIONS FOR STUDENT SERVICES, no. 135, Fall 2011 © Wiley Periodicals, Inc.
Published online in Wiley Online Library (wileyonlinelibrary.com) • DOI: 10.1002/ss.400

institution. As discussed by Braxton, Hirschy, & McClendon (2004), institutional integrity is the extent to which a college or university is true to its espoused mission and goals. It demonstrates itself when the actions of a college or university's administrators, faculty, and staff are compatible with the mission and goals proclaimed by a given college or university, and finds expression in institutional policies and rules that are administered in a fair manner.

Berger and Braxton (1998) found that fairness in the administration of institutional policies and rules influences student social integration in a positive way. Institutional integrity also manifests itself in the extent to which student expectations for college receive fulfillment. Students who experience the fulfillment of their expectations for college also experience social integration" (p. 24).

Sometimes institutions have clearly stated commitments, such as Berea College's "8 Great Commitments," but many have mission statements that consist of vague generalities. If the institutional context is clear, student affairs should be sure their own policies and practices are consistent with it. When the context is ambiguous, student affairs may need to look to the profession for guidelines to follow, a point that is discussed later.

The identity of student affairs and what it really stands for and should aspire to has been the subject of discussion from the Student Personnel Point of View through the CAS standards to the ACPA revised Statement of Ethical Principles and Standards. Although this discussion is sometimes heated, there is a central identity that continues throughout, well summarized by Young (1997): "Student affairs professionals have a strong tradition of values. They believe in individuals—whole, experiencing, and responsible. They believe in community. They believe in equality and justice for all people. They accept the responsibility to conserve, transmit, rectify, and expand these values so that students and colleagues will receive them even more solid and secure than they have" (p. 102). The moral purposes and virtues of student affairs are discussed by the other contributors to this volume and are outlined by Fried (1997) respecting autonomy, doing no harm, benefiting others, being just, being faithful, veracity, prudence, and benevolence. Fried also discusses the issues involved in enacting these purposes and values. In summary, there is reasonable consensus on the ideals that should compose integrity, as defined by philosophers.

An Ideal Description Based on Best Practice

A complementary approach views student affairs organizations as environments (Baird, 2005). Environments can be approached from a variety of perspectives, but the most useful in this context are the cultural approach and the human aggregate approach. The cultural approach is quite broad, but focuses on the underlying assumptions, values, and patterns of behavior within a group. The human aggregate approach is based on the concept that an environment will be shaped by the characterization of the majority of people within the environment. According to these approaches, the path to organizational integrity lies in creating a culture of integrity filled by people who demonstrate integrity in their professional roles.

What would be the characteristics of these cultures and people? The Center for Academic Integrity (1999), which originally focused on student cheating research but now considers integrity in general, identifies five characteristics: honesty, trust, fairness, respect, and responsibility. Honesty should characterize student affairs dealings with students, rationales for policies and decisions, and dealings with the public, and avoid any forms of cheating, distortion of the truth, or fraud. A student affairs unit built on trust will be consistent and impartial, keep its word and commitments, and be willing to "speak truth to power." Student affairs units should be characterized by fair treatment of students as well as fairness among staff members and other administrators based on predictability, clear expectations, and consistency and fairness in response to dishonesty. For student affairs, respect can include allowing, even encouraging, individual students as well as student groups to make their own decisions rather than having student affairs staff attempt to make decisions for them. It also means taking students' critiques and complaints seriously, and seeking student input on major decisions. A student affairs unit expects students, staff, and administrators to be ready to be responsible for their actions and policies, and, despite pressures from administrative superiors, peers, or the public, should take action against wrongdoing.

Challenges to Integrity

The five aspects of an ideal organization of integrity provide general models for practice. However, it may be more difficult for student affairs to maintain its organizational integrity when institutions are changing their missions and goals in ways that may create conflicts with the traditional goals of student affairs. Higher education systems and universities are in a period in which they are redefining their relationship with society. A combination of forces, including declining governmental support, changing societal expectations, and globalization, has led to a more entrepreneurial stance in academe. Characterized as commercialization (Bok, 2003), academic capitalism (Slaughter & Leslie, 1997; Slaughter & Rhoades, 2004), and responsiveness (Tierney, 1999), this stance has led to internal and external changes (Etzkowitz, Webster, & Healey, 1998; Priest & St. John, 2006). In general, these changes involve market-like behaviors on the part of institutions and faculty (Slaughter & Leslie, 1997). Various analyses have concerned the consequences of these behaviors for individual staff, institutional reward structures, management models, and external relations (e.g., Rhoades & Sporn, 2002). However, the consequences for student affairs have not been thoroughly examined.

NEW DIRECTIONS FOR STUDENT SERVICES • DOI: 10.1002/ss

One of the key changes is in the shift in expectations for funding. Although most clearly seen in the sciences, all parts of universities are increasingly encouraged to seek external funding for projects or programs as much as possible. External funders have their own agendas and expectations. At the very least, they expect to be recognized for their contribution; at the worst, they seek to control the activities of the projects. Further, external funding can have unintended consequences. For example, the sale of "pouring rights" by which only a particular soft drink company's products are available on campus is seen by some students as a sign that their institution cares little for their freedom of choice, and is viewed as petty money grubbing. A related phenomenon is the view that all activities of an administrative unit should be evaluated in terms of their outcomes in finance or prestige. This creates pressures on student affairs to produce evidence that its activities affect, albeit indirectly, the retention of tuition-paying students or result in positive publicity. Programs designed to help students in controversial areas, such as Islamic students or lesbian, gay, bisexual, or transgender (LGBT) students, may be viewed as less valuable.

The same corporate budgetary approach can lead to units competing with other units for parts of the institutional budget. Not only does this make collaboration more complicated, but it creates pressures to make programs appear successful. One way to do this is to promote positive publicity in the form of students' testimonial stories and avoid the kind of assessment recommended by Roberts and Banta.

These challenges to the integrity of student affairs programs will not disappear and show every sign of increasing. In response, student affairs must reaffirm its central commitment to student welfare. As discussed by Braxton et al. (2004):

> This construct manifests itself as an institution's abiding concern for the growth and development of its students. An institution committed to the welfare of its students also clearly communicates the high value it places on students in groups as well as individuals. The equal treatment of students and respect for them as individuals constitute additional aspects of this construct ... [which includes] the valuing of students, respect for students as individuals, and equal treatment of students spring from findings that suggest that fairly administering policies and rules (Berger & Braxton, 1998), communicating institutional policies and requirements (Berger & Braxton, 1998), and providing students with an opportunity to participate in the decision-making process about institutional rules and policies (Berger & Braxton, 1998) (pp. 22–23).

Enhancing Integrity in Student Affairs

Student affairs professionals' ability to influence the ethical and moral development of students depends on their own status as moral exemplars.

How can colleges and student affairs divisions be organized to enhance this integrity? The combinations of more complexity without clear norms, relatively low salaries for staff, limited public transparency for many day-to-day decisions, greater expectations and lowered resources, and competition lead to many challenges to integrity. One traditional response is to create and enforce codes of conduct and compliance programs. An approach that seems to be more useful is to create cultures of integrity.

Many colleges and universities rely on codes of conduct and compliance programs, which include elements of written standards, communication, monitory and auditing, and corrective action. However, they are often so loosely interpreted and enforced that they have not been highly effective. In the corporate arena, similar results led to the Sarbanes-Oxley Act, which includes, among other things, the creation of an oversight board to oversee auditing and enforcement of standards, requiring senior executives to take responsibility for the accuracy and completeness of financial reports, and penalties for manipulating, destroying, or altering records. Some institutions of higher education have adopted the fiscal oversight procedures mapped out in the act, and beefed up codes of conduct and procedures for monitoring misconduct. Some have established ethics offices, in some cases as a result of state mandate (Illinois and Minnesota), or as an institutional initiative (Dartmouth, CUNY, and UNLV). Another practice is to establish whistleblower hot lines (Florida, Texas A&M, Iowa, and Auburn). Finally, the Association of College and University Auditors has joined with Ethics Point to form a strategic Alliance to Advance Ethics and Compliance Best Practices for Higher Education, which offers consulting and software to higher education institutions.

As important as these formal efforts at compliance are, research suggests that they are not entirely successful. This is partly due to the competing views of federal sources, institutional purposes, contractual relations, and the social contracts colleges have with their constituencies. In addition, institutional values must deal with the expectations and guidelines of such groups as the American Association of University Professors (AAUP), the National Collegiate Athletic Association (NCAA), the National Association of College and University Business Officers (NACUBO), and the National Association of Student Personnel Administrators (NASPA). With this swirl of competing views, staff, including student affairs professionals, may have to rely on their own sense of integrity in day-to-day activities. However, a culture or climate of integrity can be created that can make this work more consistent and thoughtful.

Creating a Culture of Integrity

As Bertram Gallant, Beesemyer, and Kezar (2009) point out, focusing on controlling individual behavior does not lead to a culture of integrity. Rather, they recommend a number of steps to change the culture, which can be applied to student affairs divisions. These include:

NEW DIRECTIONS FOR STUDENT SERVICES • DOI: 10.1002/ss

1. Making integrity part of the mission and values statements of the division, and to regularly discuss issues of integrity and ethics in meetings as they apply to day-to-day resources.
2. Senior administrators should examine their reward structures to see if they support or undermine a culture of integrity. For example, if a priority is placed on the number of students seen per month in the counseling or career services offices rather than on the quality of the services provided, the key values of those offices may be undermined. Leaders of integrity will correct these problems.
3. Ensuring that the psychological contract between the institution and its constituents is kept is critical. For example, if staff are hired with promised job duties and benefits, those should be provided.
4. Ways to strengthen people's identification with the university and its norms should be sought. Values statements should be reinforced with specific references to job expectations and evaluation criteria. For example, at Cornell, compensation is tied to individual and team performance and contributions to the university's missions. At Iowa State, 13.9 percent of the job evaluation is based on "Impact on Institutional Mission." A specific example is found at the University of California, where each staff member is rated on performance of the Principles of Community.
5. To help staff deal with competing governmental, institutional, and professional codes, institutions or divisions can create a chart showing their areas of agreement and possible incongruence. This can be the basis of discussions that can alert constituents about issues that may affect their work.
6. The institution or division can conduct an ethical audit, which will identify rewards and perceptions about the climate for integrity. Harris and Bastedo (2011) give an example of an ethical audit, which includes items such as the receipt of honoraria or consulting fees from public officials or real and prospective business partners, and the provision of integrity training procedures for enforcing violations of codes. Areas requiring attention can be identified by examining the personal priorities and levels of integrity of individuals, units, and institutional policies. The effectiveness of integrity audits is discussed at Annual Higher Education Conferences organized by the Society of Corporate Compliance and Ethics.

These activities can be the basis for organizing training programs to produce staff and divisions of integrity.

Integrating Integrity Into Graduate Training

Although there are various approaches to the training of graduate students (Antony & Taylor, 2004), the most frequently used model describes a process of socialization to an ultimate professional role, which involves learning the specialized knowledge, skills, attitudes, values, and norms of the profession (Anderson, 1998; Baird, 1990). However, various studies (Golde & Dore, 2004; Wulff, Austin, & Associates, 2004) suggest that graduate education is only partly successful in this effort, because the skills, attitudes, and expectations are only sporadically articulated. More to the point, the assumptions of graduate education, articulated or not, often do not correspond to the changing conditions of academic and professional work (Rip & Schot, 2002). Not the least of these changes involves the ethical decisions graduates will face in a market-driven higher education system (Anderson, 2003; Ziman, 2003). The lack of organizational structures to deal with these decisions places the responsibility for ethical behavior on personal self-regulation (Braxton & Baird, 2001).

Graduate students in student affairs receive considerable training in professional ethics through courses such as "Student Affairs as a Profession" or "Case Studies in Student Affairs," and, of course, they become familiar with the theories of moral and ethical development. However, much of this training focuses on working with students as individuals or in groups, and being a responsible professional within a student affairs unit. However, many of the challenges to both individual and organizational integrity come from the external and internal pressures to be more responsive to market forces discussed earlier.

Given these changes, two general categories of skill and issues requiring ethical consideration can be discerned: entrepreneurial and intrapreneurial (Clark, 2004). These skills and issues are already part of the graduate socialization process in some fields, particularly scientific and technical fields (Henkel, 2005). However, they have not been analyzed previously within the framework of the move to market-like behaviors. Entrepreneurial skills and issues include obtaining contracts, cooperating with the business industry, and consulting. Although many academics and researchers in some fields have had to obtain external support for their activities for years, the changes in the university require them to be much more entrepreneurial, and an increasing percentage of professionals in other fields, including student affairs, face the expectation that they will seek external support. Usually, there is little systematic graduate training for the skill of writing original proposals, responding to requests for proposals, negotiating terms, and fulfilling the terms of contracts. Clearly, these involve awareness of legal and ethical issues that should be a part of training in student affairs.

Likewise, although there are some exceptions, most graduate training does not prepare students for partnerships with business and industry. Industry has a different agenda from colleges and universities, with a much greater emphasis on application, product development, and proprietary interests. Graduate students need to be prepared for these different expectations and provided with strategies for satisfying both in ethically appropriate ways (Spier, 1998). Consulting has also become a larger part of academic life, and graduate students should be prepared for working productively with clients.

As activities and projects become more complex and involve more institutional support, the intrapreneurial skills needed to obtain that support have become very important. Graduate students in student affairs sometimes have only haphazard experiences with the intricate bureaucracies of universities. University research offices, review boards, and academic officers are often involved in supporting the preparation of proposals and ensuring that the institutional infrastructure will enable the project. Thus, obtaining internal support has become a critical skill. Likewise, as more work involves cross-disciplinary teams, the skills in forming internal alliances are important. The kinds of collaboration skills needed to do this are important and should be part of graduate training in student affairs.

The changes described involve changing ethical concerns and, consequently, the training of graduate students in student affairs. Graduate students are usually carefully prepared to be concerned with such issues as fabrication of data, informed consent, and so on. However, new issues are emerging as the contract between society and higher education changes (Packham & Tasker, 1997; Slaughter & Rhoades, 2004). Graduate students must be prepared to address conflicting ethical expectations and pressures that will face them in their careers (Braxton & Baird, 2001). Graduate programs in student affairs and the professional associations need to explicate these pressures and the appropriate responses to them in graduate training in order to maintain organizational integrity in the future.

Specifically, courses such as the introduction to student affairs, issues in administrative practices, legal issues, practica, and capstone courses can focus on providing students instruction in becoming sensitive to issues of integrity, bases for evaluating the best course of action, and developing a coherent, defensible foundation for practice (Sork, 2009). This instruction can use cases created by the instructor or brought to class by students confronted with decisions in their assistantships. Then the framework of questions developed by Nash (2002) can be applied, resulting in what he calls a "moral brief":

1. Why is this case a moral dilemma?
2. What are the choices in conflict?
3. Who are the morally relevant actors?
4. Where does the action take place? Is the "where" morally relevant?
5. When does the action take place? Is the "when" morally relevant?
6. How is the manner or style of action morally relevant?
7. What are some foreseeable consequences of each decision?
8. What are some foreseeable principles involved in each decision?
9. What are some viable alternatives?

NEW DIRECTIONS FOR STUDENT SERVICES • DOI: 10.1002/ss

10. What does the code of ethics say?
11. What is your decision? (p. 117)

Students are then asked to analyze their decisions using the following questions:

1. What is your decision A? What is your decision B? (where A and B represent alternatives under consideration in no particular order of preference)
2. What *rules* do you appeal to in order to justify (support, give reasons for) each of the decisions?
3. What *principles* do you appeal to in order to justify each of the decisions?
4. What *theories* do you appeal to in order to justify each of the decisions?
5. What *conclusions* do you reach regarding your final decision after you compare both justifications?
6. What afterthoughts do you have now that you have made your final decision?

Although this systematic examination of issues and the responses to them requires time, the resulting improvement in dealing with the complex, multidimensional problems in student affairs is well worth it.

Conclusion

By considering what we mean by integrity, identifying the challenges to integrity in practice, creating cultures of integrity, and preparing graduate students for the decisions they will make in their careers, we can make student affairs stronger and resilient in a time of challenges.

References

Anderson, M. S. (ed.). *The Experience of Being in Graduate School: An Exploration.* San Francisco: Jossey-Bass, 1998.

Anderson, M. S. "The Role of Scientific Associations in Promoting Research Integrity and Deterring Research Misconduct." *Science and Engineering Ethics*, 2003, 9(2), 269–272.

Antony, J. S. and Taylor, E. "Theories and Strategies of Academic Career Socialization: Improving Paths to the Professoriate for Black Graduate Students." In D. H. Wulff, E. A. Austin and Associates (eds.), *Paths to the Professoriate: Strategies for Enriching the Preparation of Future Faculty.* San Francisco: Jossey-Bass, 2004.

Baird, L. L. "The Melancholy of Anatomy: The Personal and Professional Development of Graduate and Professional School Students." In J. C. Smart (ed.), *Higher Education: Handbook of Theory and Research*, Vol. 6. New York: Agathon Press, 1990.

Baird, L. L. "College Environments and Climates: Assessments and Their Theoretical Assumptions. In J.C. Smart (ed.), *Higher Education: Handbook of Theory and Research*, Vol. 20. Norwell, MA: Springer, 2005.

Berger, J. B., and Braxton, J.M. "Revising Tinto's Interactionalist Theory of Student Departure Through Theory Elaboration: Examining the Role of Organizational Attributes in the Persistence Process." *Research in Higher Education*, 1998, *39*, 109–119.

Bertram Gallant, T., Beesemyer, L. A., & Kezar, A. "A Culture of Ethics in Hgher Education." In D. Segal & J. Knapp (eds.), *The Business of Higher Education*. Westport, CT: Greenwood Publishing Group, 2009.

Bok, D. C. Universities in the Marketplace: The Commercialization of Higher Education. Princeton, NJ: Princeton University Press, 2003.

Braxton, J. M. and Baird, L. L. "Preparation for Professional Self-regulation." *Science and Engineering Ethics*, 2001, *7*(4), 593–610.

Braxton, J. M., Hirschy, A. S., and MClendon, S. A. *Understanding and Reducing Student Departure*. San Francisco: Wiley. ASHE-ERIC Higher Education Report, 2004.

Center for Academic Integrity. *The Fundamental Values of Academic Integrity*. Des Plaines, IL: Center for Academic Integrity, 1999.

Clark, B.R. *Sustaining Change in Universities: Continuities in Case Studies and Concepts*. Maidenhead, England; New York: Society for Research into Higher Education and Open University Press, 2004.

Cox, D., LaCaze, M., & Levine, M. (2008). Integrity. In *Stanford Encyclopedia of Philosophy*. Retrieved from http://plato.stanford.edu/entries/integrity.

Etzkowitz, H., Webster, A., & Healey, P. (Eds.). *Capitalizing Knowledge: New Intersections of Industry and Academia*. Albany, NY: State University of New York Press, 1998.

Fried, J. (ed.). *Ethics for Today's Campus: New Perspectives on Education, Student Development, and Institutional Management. New Directions in Student Services*, No. 77. San Francisco, CA: Jossey-Bass, 1997.

Golde, C. M., and Dore, T. M. "The Survey of Doctoral Education and Career Preparation: The Importance of Disciplinary Contexts." In D.H. Wulff, E.A. Austin, and Associates. *Paths to the Professoriate: Strategies for Enriching the Preparation of Future Faculty*. San Francisco: Jossey-Bass, 2004.

Henkel, M. "Academic Identity and Autonomy in a Changing Policy Environment." *Higher Education*, 2005, *49*(1–2), 155–176.

Nash, R. *"Real World" Ethics: Frameworks for Educators and Human Service Professionals. Professional Ethics in Education Series*, 11. New York, NY: Teachers College Press, 2002.

Packham, D., and Tasker, M. "Industry and the Academy—a Faustian Contract?" *Industry and Higher Education*, 1997, *11*(2), 85–90.

Priest, D. M., and St. John, E. P. (eds.). *Privatization and Public Universities*. Bloomington: Indiana University Press, 2006.

Rhoades, G., and Sporn, B. "Quality Assurance in Europe and the U.S.: Professional and Political Economic Framing of Higher Education Policy." *Higher Education*, 2002, *43*(3), 355–390.

Rip, A., and Schot, J. W. "Identifying Loci for Influencing the Dynamics of Technological Development." In K.H. Sorenson and R. Williams (eds.), *Shaping Technology, Guiding Policy: Concepts, Spaces and Tools*. Cheltenham, UK; Northampton, MA: Elgar, 2002.

Slaughter, S., and Leslie, L. L. *Academic Capitalism: Politics, Policies, and the Entrepreneurial University*. Baltimore: Johns Hopkins University Press, 1997.

Slaughter, S., and Rhoades, G. *Academic Capitalism and the New Economy: Markets, State, and Higher Education*. Baltimore: Johns Hopkins University Press, 2004.

Sork, T. "Applied Ethics in Adult and Continuing Education Literature." In E. Burge (ed.), *Negotiating Ethical Practice in Adult Education. New Directions for Adult and Continuing Education*, No. 123. San Francisco, CA: Jossey-Bass, 2009.

Spier, R. E. "Ethics and the Funding of Research and Development at Universities." *Science and Engineering Ethics*, 1998, 4(3), 375–384.

Tierney, W. G. *Building the Responsive Campus: Creating High Performance Colleges and Universities.* Thousand Oaks, CA: Sage, 1999.

Williams, B. *Moral Luck: Philosophical Papers 1973–1980.* Cambridge: Cambridge University Press, 1981.

Wulff, D. H., Austin, A.E., and Associates. *Paths to the Professoriate: Strategies for Enriching the Preparation of Future Faculty.* San Francisco: Jossey-Bass, 2004.

Young, R. "Guiding Values and Philosophy." In S. Komives & D. Woodard (eds.), *Student Services: A Handbook for the Profession*, 3rd edition. San Francisco, CA: Jossey-Bass, 1997.

Ziman, J. M. "Non-instrumental Roles of Science." *Science and Engineering Ethics*, 2003, 9, 17–27.

LEONARD BAIRD *is a professor in the School of Educational Policy and Leadership, The Ohio State University, and executive editor of the* Journal of Higher Education.

3

*The Council for the Advancement of Standards in Higher
Education (CAS) has created standards that can be used
to increase structural soundness and ethical excellence in
institutional programs and services.*

Promoting Integrity through Standards of Practice

Susan R. Komives and Jan Arminio

For over 30 years, the Council for the Advancement of Standards in Higher
Education (CAS) has developed and promulgated standards of practice for
quality programs and services. The standards are designed intentionally to
promote student learning and developmental outcomes through a self-
assessment process. CAS has coalesced professional expectations from 40
member associations, emphasizing the integrity of campus programs
through comprehensive structural soundness and ethical excellence.

It is indeed appropriate that a chapter on standards of practice be
included in a book describing professional integrity. There are two related
uses of the word *integrity*. One refers to a commitment to values, standards,
and ethical principles. The other use refers to "a condition of being undi-
vided," referring to being complete or whole (Merriam-Webster.com, 2011).
These two definitions connect in this chapter in that integrity demands that
student affairs professionals commit to and are united with standards of
practice and ethics of the profession. The CAS standards are the standards
with which student affairs professionals are expected to unite.

An example may assist in appreciating the role CAS can play in creating a student affairs environment of integrity. This example will be developed over the course of this chapter. Chris has advocated for the creation
of an LGBT Center and approval has been granted at this midsized institution to establish such a center. In trying to ensure that a quality center is
conceived, Chris turns to CAS and its resources for guidance. We shall
make references to Chris and this new opportunity as we describe how CAS
assists in ensuring integrity.

New Directions for Student Services, no. 135, Fall 2011 © Wiley Periodicals, Inc.
Published online in Wiley Online Library (wileyonlinelibrary.com) • DOI: 10.1002/ss.401

We start with a review of the role of standards in professional practice, addressing how the CAS approach is foundational to the integrity of quality professional practice. Then, our discussion moves to the various CAS resources that ground student affairs practice in integrity. Specifically, these include the CAS General Standards, the CAS Statement of Shared Ethical Principles, and CAS Characteristics of Individual Excellence for Professional Practice in Higher Education. Our chapter ends by exploring challenges CAS faces to ensure quality programs in student affairs.

Role of Standards in Professional Practice

In the example introduced earlier, Chris seeks to use standards to become informed about critical components of a quality LGBT Center, a new program at the institution, and his new responsibilities. Professional standards provide an instrument to aid in the design of quality programs and services. Standards also provide an exemplar that professionals can use to judge the quality of their work.

More specifically, standards serve to explicate expectations to new professionals and guide professionals in creating new programs, improving existing programs, and accepting new responsibilities. By facilitating comparisons, these uses of standards promote professional self-regulation. Meeting standards helps assure service users (e.g., students, their families, faculty) of the integrity and soundness of the professional practices with whom they are engaging.

Self-Regulation.   Establishing standards has become critical to the public trust of professions. In the extreme, government regulatory agencies use standards from a field (e.g., medicine) to regulate that field, accredit preparation programs, and license or credential practitioners such as doctors or nurses. This protects the public when securing medical services or practices. Even when professions do not accredit programs or individuals are not licensed, self-regulation is critical for public trust. Standards can prevent or moderate outside intervention in professional concerns.

Standards related to higher education are relatively new. They differ from professional standards in lower educational levels in several ways. First, standards in higher education have mainly served to improve educational practices rather than to influence degree attainment. Second, there has been less public scrutiny because higher education attendance is not mandatory. Historically, "there were relatively few colleges and universities, only a small portion of the population attended, and the curriculum was not of concern to many" (Alstete, 2004, p. 7). Finally, it has only been recently that the public trust in higher education has been questioned (U.S. Department of Education, 2006) whereas the K–12 sector has been scrutinized for decades. Because of the question of public trust, some states and institutions have tied funding requests to performance standards.

NEW DIRECTIONS FOR STUDENT SERVICES • DOI: 10.1002/ss

History of Standards in Student Affairs

Standards and accreditation began at the end of the 19th century and were seen as a response to inconsistency and confusion regarding college admission. "Because the federal government lacked the authority to deal with the unresolved educational issues that were beyond the scope of state officials" college officials began to solve the problem of inconsistencies themselves (Alstete, 2004, p. 7). Therefore, regional school accrediting associations began to set minimal standards for the accreditation of higher education institutions (Alstete, 2004). Subsequently, Andrew Carnegie established the Carnegie Foundation for the Advancement of Teaching, which required institutions to comply with national "minimal standards" regarding faculty, courses, and admission requirements in order to be funded (Alstete, 2004, p. 9). These beginnings enabled students to transfer from one institution to another, adding consistency and credibility to that process. And from these beginnings accreditation came to be defined as a systematized process for an established formalized authoritative body to recognize institutions that have met a prescribed level of performance (Mable, 1991).

After admission standards were formalized for postsecondary institutions, specialized discipline standards such as counseling and college health were established and promulgated along with generalized institutional standards (Alstete, 2004). However, the accreditation system has been criticized for most of its history. Some educators have disliked the notion of outsiders dictating institutional policies, ridiculed the cost in terms of time and money, lamented the competition it encourages, disparaged a loss of innovation and creativity, and described the accreditation process as self-serving (Alstete, 2004). Accreditation was criticized as well for being "elusive, nebulous, superficial, and meaning different things to different people" (p. 17). Most recently, the Center for College Affordability and Productivity called for the complete overhaul of the current accreditation process (Kelderman, 2010).

Student affairs emphasized self-assessment instead of accreditation through the Council for the Advancement of Standards in Higher Education (CAS) that was created in 1979. In recent years, assessment in higher education has expanded beyond its original purposes to include assessment for comparability (i.e., benchmarking against other institutions), assessment for accountability (i.e., holding offices responsible for some level of outcome), and assessment for improvement (i.e., providing data to make evidence-based decisions to make programs more effective). The CAS approach advocates for self-assessment for the purpose of improvement.

CAS, a consortium of professional associations in higher education, published its first set of standards in 1986. The standards covered a broad span of educational programs and services such as academic advising; campus activities; career services; disability support services; health promotion services; lesbian, gay, bisexual, and transgender programs; and others.

From the start, the credibility of CAS standards was based on inter-association consensus about the essential qualities of student development programs and services, as well as for graduate school education of professionals entering student affairs (CAS, 1980). Subsequent compilations of standards were published in 1997, 1999, 2001, 2003, 2006, and 2009.

The CAS standards reflect the evolution of student affairs administration as a professional field. Establishing standards is necessary in any profession, so the creation of standards was a natural progression in student affairs (Paterson & Carpenter, 1989). Indeed, Paterson and Carpenter (1989) stated that CAS standards represented "a major step forward in the efforts toward becoming a profession" (p. 125). Furthermore, in recent years, government agencies and the public have sought to hold institutions more accountable for student learning, and assessment has become pertinent to accreditation (Upcraft & Schuh, 1996). CAS standards represent the student affairs profession's commitment to set its own standards and inform others outside the profession about its purpose, values, and goals. By establishing standards, "Student affairs clearly announced its determination to control its own destiny" (Bryan & Mullendore, 1991, p. 29) and assure the integrity of the field. CAS standards are "evolving documents" (p. 29) in that they are revised every five to seven years, and new standards are being written continuously. In 2010, CAS made new or newly revised standards available on its web site in between the publication the CAS book of standards.

Uses of CAS Standards

Standards can be used for program development, continuous improvement, self-study for accreditation or internal review, staff development, student development, program planning, program evaluation, acceptance of and education about student affairs services and programs, identification of student learning and developmental outcomes, political maneuverability, budgetary assistance, ethical practice, and to standardize language in functional areas (Arminio & Gochenauer, 2004; Bryan & Mullendore, 1991). Plus, they provide "criteria by which programs of professional preparation can be judged" (Miller, 1991, p. 48). Following are ways these standards address integrity in student affairs practice.

Specific Ways CAS Standards Address Integrity

Elements of Standards.   A comprehensive program design is promoted in each standard that assures the structural soundness, wholeness, and integrity. Each CAS standard is comprised of 14 categories of general standards that are consistent across each of the 40 functional area standards. The categories of general standards are (1) mission, (2) program, (3) leadership, (4) human resources, (5) ethics, (6) legal responsibilities, (7) equity and access, (8) diversity, (9) organization and management, (10) campus and external relations, (11) financial resources, (12) technology, (13) facilities and equipment, and (14) assessment and evaluation. Since these general standards are consistent in each functional area, entire divisions of student affairs can be consistent in their approaches.

The word *standard* was first used in western Germany in the 12th century to describe a "flag or conspicuous object as a rallying point" (Harper, 2010). Literally, standard meant to stand hard or firm. As a result, CAS standards are written as "must" or "shall" statements. Programs and services are required to meet these "must" or "shall" statements unless a review team can verify that the standard is met by another functional area within the institution. "Shall" or "can" statements, called *guidelines*, are descriptors of ways to enhance program quality beyond the essential components. Programs may select those guideline elements they wish to assess based on their program and institution.

In returning to our example, the reader can see how Chris would utilize standards and guidelines as information inputs to guide the creation of the LGBT program and service. From writing the LGBT Center mission to aligning the mission with essential aspects of the program, collaborating with campus and community agencies, and assessing program outcomes, the CAS standards advance the wholeness and consistency of the LGBT program integrity.

A Focus on Ethics.   Integrity has an ethical dimension and the CAS process explicitly expects and promotes ethical professional behavior. The CAS Preamble asserts "beliefs about ethics require that all programs and services be carried out in an environment of integrity and high ideals" (CAS, 2009, p. 18). Ethical practices are so critical that one of the 14 general standards is devoted to that expectation. See Exhibit 3.1 for specifics of the CAS Ethics general standard.

In its attempt to advance professional integrity, CAS thematized the ethical statements of member associations and identified some common denominators. "From these codes, CAS has created a statement of shared ethical principles that focuses on seven basic principles that form the foundation for CAS member association codes: autonomy, non-malfeasance, beneficence, justice, fidelity, veracity, and affiliation" (CAS Book of Standards, 2009, pp. 23–24; see also www.CAS.edu). Program realities may not be what program ideals are so professional associations need to regularly revisit their professional codes of conduct to be responsive to issues such as cultural relevancy.

Chris will want to contemplate the ways that the CAS standards can be enacted through ethical means. How can this new program meet the standard of "educating the campus community when decisions or policies may affect the achievement of LGBT students" (CAS, 2009, p. 297) with veracity, beneficence, justice, and autonomy?

Individual Excellence.   CAS responded to concerns of the lack of consistent and quality supervision in student affairs (Winston & Creamer, 1997) by creating Characteristics of Individual Excellence for Professional Practice in Higher Education. These "ideal performance characteristics that describe professional practice" (CAS, 2009, p. 21) assume that integrity is a

---

Exhibit 3.1.   CAS General Standard: Ethics

Persons involved in the delivery of Programs and Services must adhere to the highest principles of ethical behavior. Programs and services must review relevant professional ethical standards and develop or adopt and implement appropriate statements of ethical practice. Programs and services must publish these statements and ensure their periodic review by relevant constituencies.

Programs and services must orient new staff members to relevant ethical standards and statements of ethical practice.

Staff members must ensure that privacy and confidentiality are maintained with respect to all communications and records to the extent that such records are protected under the law and appropriate statements of ethical practice. Information contained in students' education records must not be disclosed except as allowed by relevant laws and institutional policies. Staff members must disclose to appropriate authorities information judged to be of an emergency nature, especially when the safety of the individual or others is involved, or when otherwise required by institutional policy or relevant law.

Staff members must be aware of and comply with the provisions contained in the institution's policies pertaining to human subjects research and student rights and responsibilities, as well as those in other relevant institutional policies addressing ethical practices and confidentiality of research data concerning individuals.

Staff members must recognize and avoid personal conflicts of interest or appearance thereof in the performance of their work.

Staff members must strive to insure the fair, objective, and impartial treatment of all persons with whom they interact.

When handling institutional funds, staff members must ensure that such funds are managed in accordance with established and responsible accounting procedures and the fiscal policies or processes of the institution.

Promotional and descriptive information must be accurate and free of deception.

Staff members must perform their duties within the limits of their training, expertise, and competence. When these limits are exceeded, individuals in need of further assistance must be referred to persons possessing appropriate qualifications.

Staff members must use suitable means to confront and otherwise hold accountable other staff members who exhibit unethical behavior.

Staff members must be knowledgeable about and practice ethical behavior in the use of technology.

Source: Council for the Advancement of Standards in Higher Education. (2009). *CAS professional standards for higher education* (7th ed., pp. 32–33). Washington, DC: Author. Reprinted with permission.

---

lifelong endeavor shared by the individual as well as the institution at which the professional is employed. To illustrate, self-mastery characteristics include a commitment to excellence of all work, utilizing self-reflection to improve practice, viewing professionalism as an important aspect of personal identity, maintaining position-appropriate appearance, managing one's personal life so that overall professional effectiveness is maintained, assuming accountability for mistakes, and reevaluating continued employment when personal, professional, and institutional goals are incompatible and inhibit the purist of excellence.

Chris might decide to use these characteristics for self-development and self-evaluation purposes, by reflecting on evidence of how these characteristics are met. Where are there gaps? Chris can also contemplate how to embed these characteristics in a performance evaluation process.

CAS Challenges

Intentional professional practice guides the process through which standards are established and inform how standards are modified. However, CAS must balance the demand for high quality with the realities of practice. Criticisms have been voiced that the standards are too prescriptive, are based on inputs rather than on outcomes, and are not available for free (W. Barrett, personal communication, June 5, 2002; Love, 2000). The graduate preparation program standards have been criticized for not allowing institutional programs to express their unique nature (Love, 2000). In responding to feedback such as this, CAS has upheld integrity through transparency, dialogue, and working continually to improve standards to guide practice.

How standards influence effective practice is another challenge. Creamer (2003) called for a study of the effects of CAS standards and guidelines on student learning and development. Among other questions, he asked, "Are educational programs and services that are guided by CAS standards and guidelines more effective than similar programs and services that are not guided by CAS standards and guidelines?" (p. 119). There are efforts currently to confirm this connection.

Perhaps the biggest challenge is the promulgation of standards. The standards have not been fully integrated into preparation and practice. Although most student affairs graduate programs teach about the standards and many professional associations have regular CAS convention programs, many higher education graduate programs do not teach about CAS. In addition, few professionals know about CAS if they come to student affairs from other disciplines. CAS has created a new strategic outreach agenda to address these challenges.

Conclusion

CAS provides professional guidance to develop quality programs and practices that result in intentional student learning outcomes. Comprehensive

NEW DIRECTIONS FOR STUDENT SERVICES • DOI: 10.1002/ss

standards and the self-assessment process assure the sustainability and integrity of professionally intentional program design. Student affairs administrators can depend on CAS for timely and thoughtful guidance bringing structural soundness and ethical excellence to professional practice.

References

Alstete, J. W. "Accreditation Matters: Achieving Academic Recognition and Renewal." *ASHE-ERIC Higher Education Report: Vol. 30*, Number 4. San Francisco, CA: Wiley, 2004.

Arminio, J., and Gochenauer, P. "After 16 Years of Publishing Standards, Do CAS Standards Make a Difference?" *College Student Affairs Journal*, 2004, *24*, 51–65.

Bryan, W., and Mullendore, R. "Operationalizing CAS Standards for Program Evaluation and Planning." In W. Bryan, R. Winston, Jr., and T. K. Miller (Eds.), *Using Professional Standards in Student Affairs. New Directions for Student Services*, 53. San Francisco, CA: Jossey-Bass, 1991.

Council for the Advancement of Standards. By-laws, 1980.

Council for the Advancement of Standards in Higher Education. *CAS Professional Standards for Higher Education* (7th ed.). Washington, DC: Author, 2009.

Creamer, D. G. "Research Needed on the Use of CAS Standards and Guidelines." *College Student Affairs Journal*, 2003, 22, 109–124.

Harper, D. Online etymology dictionary, 2010. Retrieved on June 19, 2011, from http://etymonline.com/index.php?search=standards$searchmode=term.

Kelderman, E. "Center Renews Call for Overhaul of Nation's Accreditation System," 2010. *Chronicle of Higher Education*. Retrieved on October 20, 2010, from http://chronicle.com/article/Center-Renews-Call-for/125017/.

Love, P. "Report on the Feedback Received About the CAS Self-Assessment Guide and Process." Unpublished manuscript, August 2000.

Mable, P. "Professional Standards: An Introduction and Historical Perspective." In W. A. Bryan, R. B. Winston, Jr., and T. K. Miller (Eds.), *Using Professional Standards in Student Affairs. New Directions for Student Services*, 53. San Francisco, CA: Jossey-Bass, 1991.

Merriam-Webster.com. Integrity. *Online Dictionary*, 2011. Retrieved from http://www.merriam-webster.com/dictionary/integrity?show=0&t=1308574535

Miller, T. K. "Using Standards in Professional Preparation." In W. A. Bryan, R. B. Winston, Jr., and T. K. Miller (Eds.), *Using Professional Standards in Student Affairs. New Directions for Student Services*, 53. San Francisco: Jossey-Bass, 1991.

Paterson, B., and Carpenter, S. "The Emerging Student Affairs Profession: What Still Needs to Be Done." *NASPA Journal*, 1989, 27, 123–127.

Upcraft, M. L., and Schuh, J. H. *Assessment in Student Affairs: A Guide for Practitioners*. San Francisco, CA: Jossey-Bass, 1996.

U.S. Department of Education. *A Test of Leadership: Charting the Future of U.S. Higher Education*. Washington, DC.: Author, 2006.

Winston, R. B., and Creamer, D. G., Jr. *Improving Staffing Practices in Student Affairs*. San Francisco, CA: Jossey-Bass, 1997.

SUSAN R. KOMIVES is a professor in the Counseling and Personnel Services Department at the University of Maryland. JAN ARMINIO is a professor and chair in the Department of Counseling and College Student Personnel at Shippensburg University. Both authors have served as president of the Council for the Advancement of Standards in Higher Education.

4

Integrity is shown when the principles, procedures, structure, communication, and assessment of our student transactions are clear, consistent, accessible, and transparent.

Integrity in Transactional Leadership

Thomas Miller

Student affairs practitioners are educated to focus on students, and at professional conferences and meetings, they learn more about how to maintain the welfare of students. However, contemporary forces challenge this training and the ability of student affairs professionals to act consistently with integrity (Kuh, Lyons, Miller, & Trow, 1994).

The welfare of students requires a singular priority of integrity in all our transactions with them. Honesty, consistency, and transparency must be maintained, despite negative forces such as limited personnel resources, goods and services, time, campus culture, and technology.

This chapter begins with a discussion of the impact of limited resources on the integrity of transactions between students and student affairs administrators. A framework and guiding principles for maintaining integrity are offered, and then some general principles for transactions with students are presented. Next, the chapter involves integrity issues associated with communication with students, including challenges of responsiveness, and how transactions may need to be adapted to individual needs and interests. After that discussion, some issues associated with honesty and accuracy are described, as well as the matter of confidentiality in our transactions with students. The challenges of problem solving with students are discussed next, and the chapter concludes with possibilities for the assessment of the integrity of transactions.

Limited Resources

Some institutions face circumstances where resource limitations or reductions threaten the integrity of transactions with students. Responsible

NEW DIRECTIONS FOR STUDENT SERVICES, no. 135, Fall 2011 © Wiley Periodicals, Inc.
Published online in Wiley Online Library (wileyonlinelibrary.com) • DOI: 10.1002/ss.402

administrators need to carefully evaluate the costs associated with reductions in the integrity of how students are treated and reflect on whether those costs are worth any savings that are associated. For example, personnel can be limited due to budget declines or institutional growth. When there are not enough people to respond to students or deliver services, mistakes can be made, misinformation can be delivered, and students can be served insufficiently or in an untimely fashion. Institutions that experience unanticipated, rapid growth may also find themselves with insufficient staffing infrastructures to manage student needs. Also, limits of fiscal resources can affect the integrity of the material goods and services with which student affairs professionals serve students. For example, being unable to fund a reprinted standard in the student handbook or mail an updated policy to all students may result in their being uninformed about and ill-prepared for a change in policy. Having insufficient funds to initiate a program directed to an underrepresented group of students may result in their frustration and feeling excluded from institutional attention.

Further, time limitations can affect how integrity issues play out in dealings with students. To illustrate, leaving students out of policy design matters can compromise integrity, but state-mandated changes in policy may give administrators insufficient time to include students in the development of procedures to accommodate the changes. The general culture of the campus might also affect the integrity with which students are served. The principle of the primacy of student welfare is a value that motivates student affairs professionals. However, some institutions face challenges associated with space, financial resources, accreditation, or academic programs where student interests can be lost or at least set aside for a time. Finally, although technological advances have increased the pace at which students can conduct transactions with institutions, technology often cannot provide the flexibility and individual support that human contacts do. An institution that relies almost exclusively on technology for service to students may find some individuals caught between institutionally expressed values of support and the reality of their experiences.

Framework and Some Guiding Principles

Bob Young, in his chapter on the forms of institutional integrity, described the notion of ethical integrity. How institutions measure themselves on integrity issues depends largely on this principle. Organizations with high levels of ethical integrity share characteristics that resonate with colleges and universities. Young cited Paine's (1997) characterization of those organizations as self-governing, responsible, morally sound, and principled. Few higher educational institutions would not embrace those characteristics and call them their own. They form a useful framework for the review of integrity issues in the college and university setting.

NEW DIRECTIONS FOR STUDENT SERVICES • DOI: 10.1002/ss

Young further described the ethical ideals associated with student affairs work, and that institutional type has an impact on those ideals. Large public universities necessarily espouse different values and claim different virtues than do small, religiously affiliated institutions. The humble virtues of faith, hope, and love are more easily embedded in the culture of the smaller private college—particularly if it is religiously affiliated—than the large public one because of the differences in their respective missions. However, if those virtues are important to the student affairs profession, as argued by Young, then institutional type forms a context for challenges to fulfill them, but not an excuse to ignore them.

An overriding principle of integrity associated with transactions with college students is the focus on the welfare and interests of the students, themselves. That focus is enhanced by transactions between institutions and students that have clarity, consistency and fairness. A necessary additional element is the design and management of those transactions. They must include full involvement by students.

General Principles

The processes of transactions are keys to ensure their integrity, more than the content of them. Those processes need to be widely regarded as having clarity and consistency, fairness and openness in any associated funding, and simplicity. As a result, these processes will be easily understood and fully disclosed to students.

Clarity and Consistency.   Institutions should work to make all of their transactional processes with students as clear and understandable as possible. Printed publications and Web pages should provide comprehensive guidance on how processes work and where students should go to seek any needed clarification, flexibility, or exception to the requirements. Many transactions with institutions are mysterious to students, and include hidden rules and processes that students encounter only in situations of need. Students can lose trust in the institution unless the transactions are associated with clarity and consistency. A few examples follow.

The process for admission to the institution should be clear. Candidates for admission should know the standards and norms for processing their applications, and those standards should be consistent over time. The time frames for institutional decision making and student commitments should be specified, reasonable, and clear.

Class registration procedures should be consistent, clear, and easy to use. If exceptions are made that enable students to register early and secure more favorable class schedules, then the process for making those exceptions should be clear, fair, and readily understood. In addition, students should be able to find sufficient options for courses that are required for their degree programs, so as to construct reasonable course schedules. If approval by faculty members or advisors is required for course registration, then those advisors should be accessible to students and participate in the registration/advising process in meaningful, helpful, ways.

The funding of student organizations gives some students the opportunity to explore how budgets work and how funds can be used to advance organizational growth and development. Decisions about organization funding should be objective, open, and fair, and the procedures should be obvious to all. Students who are responsible for organization spending should be trained and supported on institutional procedures and processes, and issues of integrity in spending should be made clear to them.

Finally, student conduct should be managed in a fair and even-handed manner. Rules and procedures should be clear, widely published, and accessible to all. Responses to allegations of student misconduct should be timely and consistent, and respect must be maintained for all of those who participate in the process.

Fairness and Openness in Funding and Fees.   Student fees for services can be established in ways that present integrity challenges if the process is not open. When a college arranges full participation by students in the establishment of fee structures, it has an opportunity to communicate a sense of fairness in the process and create an enhanced sense of trust on the part of students. However, student participation in such processes must be meaningful, informed, and real, not artificially contrived. It should be consistent as well. Consistency should be evident in the commitment to make students part of the process, and not just for some fee matters and not others. Students should know well in advance about their opportunities to participate, so they can prepare for the process adequately.

Another issue is fees that are hidden or buried in student bills so as to be hard to discern from other billing matters. When students receive their regular bills, they should know immediately what they are paying for and how much of their payment is intended to support specific departments or programs.

Some institutions have been strapped for funding and have created new service fees to generate revenue streams. When students have not been charged for counseling services, for example, institutional officials should consider carefully the impact of assessing fees for those services, particularly when students have not participated fully in the decision-making process. Charging fees for other services like campus transportation, parking, or health services, brings an equal risk to ethical integrity. Such decisions should be entered into with care and openness.

The same risk applies to fees that are increased without open conversation with students. Room and board fees are typical. The costs associated with on-campus living should be well publicized and clear to students, as should costs (and associated requirements) for on-campus dining.

Simplicity.   Students become frustrated when they have to take two or three different steps, or get two or three different signatures, to bring a

New Directions for Student Services • DOI: 10.1002/ss

transaction to completion. Most business transactions can be simplified. Larger universities, in particular, tend to have complex requirements in their transactions with students, but their students are not used to anything like that. Many of their high schools were smaller and more student friendly, as were their neighborhoods and their shopping experiences. They can view complex transactions as signs of institutional indifference, inappropriateness, or incompetence. Some examples follow where administrative processes might be simplified.

Students should have clear and easy access to transcripts of their academic records. Transcripts can be provided in a timely fashion, and students should know how long it will take to get theirs. Any fees associated with transcript production should be well publicized and reasonable.

Students should know where, when, and how to get good academic advice. Advisors should be accessible, particularly at the most important times in an academic year. The quality of the advisors' advice and relationships with students should be assessed, and training should be provided to meet different developmental and cultural needs.

Full Disclosure.   Sometimes, students are allowed to reach inaccurate conclusions about services and the circumstances under which they are provided. When institutions allow students to develop unreasonable expectations about services and associated transactions, it may be because they have not fully explained and detailed the conditions of the services and their limitations. To illustrate, when an institution promotes health service or a counseling center as "full service," a student can make inaccurate assumptions about what that term means. The parameters of services should be clear, with minimum room for incomplete or incorrect interpretations.

Other examples include residence hall room assignments, which should be guided by fair and consistent standards that students know about and understand. Changes in student conduct rules and regulations need to be publicized, as should policy adjustments and hours of operation.

Structural Concerns

When an institution's student services are challenging to navigate, their associated integrity is compromised. Student services, particularly at larger universities, can be difficult to access and understand, especially for new students. Even though it can be difficult to improve their structural elements, these services need to be located conveniently with purposes and programs that are understood by users. Otherwise, their ethical integrity as *student* services is compromised.

Accessibility.   Services need to be accessible when students need them. Students do not live nine-to-five lives, and universities need to respond to their actual day-to-day schedules. Additionally, schools should weigh the fairness of basing student access to services and programs on their residence. Resident students can have a vastly greater chance to receive services and participate in programs than nonresidents, such as many adult and graduate students who come to campus in the evening. Universal access is impossible, but equitable access has more integrity than restricted access.

Access issues play out differently in different functional areas. For example, many students need access to learning support for their coursework, which should be available when students need it the most, often in evenings and on weekends, and in convenient locations.

Timely Access.   Students generally exist in "now" time. They have immediate access to research over the Internet, and they can get cash at an ATM without leaving their cars. This is the world they know, and there are times when they are frustrated by institutions that delay responses to their concerns. An amount of time that seems reasonable to an administrator can seem unreasonable to a student who has to wait for a refund from an overpayment of a bill or for an appointment with an advisor for a change in a class schedule. Ethical integrity is at risk when institutions do not do their best to accommodate students in as timely a manner as possible. For example, the same amount of time should be required to pay a fine for parking as to receive a credit when the violation is successfully appealed. When institutions are fast in meeting their own needs and slow in responding to student interests, they need to modify structures instead of jeopardizing their integrity.

Affordability and Values.   The cost for services should be closely evaluated, and institutions should make substantial efforts to see that costs do not deprive financially needy students from access to services due to cost. If costs are high, then they need to be assessed, justified, and explained. For example, when different food options are available, the nutritional values of food items should be clear to students, and educational materials about dining options and nutrition should be made available. Student feedback about dining services should be solicited, and students should be invited to participate in planning about food offerings and dining programs. The same could be said for campus housing, parking, and other services for which there is an associated fee.

Locations and Values.   Services need to be located in places where students can conveniently access them. That includes psychological as well as physical location. For example, the services to support student mental health should be centrally located, available to students at the times they need them, and situated to protect the confidentiality needs of students who want to use them.

Parking should be readily accessible for students. Lots should be well lit, and transportation should be available from any remote location. Fees for parking and for on-campus transportation should be weighed against value and understood by users, and student input should be part of the process in the establishment of fees.

NEW DIRECTIONS FOR STUDENT SERVICES • DOI: 10.1002/ss

Some operations are located for the convenience of administrators instead of students. The location of security dispatchers or information technology services might be evaluated in this regard, as might continuing education centers, foundation and fund-raising centers, alumni operations, and distance learning services.

Communication Concerns

An institution might benefit by evaluating how often and in what forms it communicates with students. Standardized patterns of communication keep students informed and involved in general institutional matters. The forms of communication may matter less than the process, but regular updates about key deadlines, policy matters, or general advisories help students recognize that they are full participants in the institutional community.

Conversely, institutions should assess how they encourage and facilitate communication from students, the extent to which it is simple, and its various forms. Inviting students to express concerns and praise associated with their experiences can inform practice and assist the institution to be responsive and engaged in student welfare.

Staff Responsiveness. First responders, the people who greet students who want to initiate transactions, are crucial to the integrity of student affairs. Training is essential to their success. These staff members need to be (1) sensitive to students and any distress that they may feel, and (2) knowledgeable about the functions of other departments, so they can make accurate referrals when necessary. These skills add an atmosphere of ethical caring to the improvement of efficient and timely service.

Adaptable to Individual Interests and Needs. Maintaining a consistent approach to standards, rules, and deadlines is essential to transactional integrity, but occasions arise when unique conditions and needs require procedural flexibility. Decision makers need to be authorized to make adjustments in processes when they recognize the need to adapt to these circumstances, and strategies that incorporate it into decision making can guide responses to extraordinary circumstances. Consistency is necessary, and consistent sensitivity to unique needs is defensible practice.

Individual interests play out in virtually all student affairs functional areas. For example, individually focused career counseling support must always be available, while its career and academic aspects are coordinated in coherent ways by academic advisors and career counselors. The same respect for individual needs and service coordination can be applied to counseling and health services.

The Student as Partner. Students should be included in discussions about changes in policies and procedures that govern how transactions are engaged. Student participation involves the recipients of services in their delivery. It creates an atmosphere of ethical engagement and builds acceptance for final decisions, even when administrative convenience or budget concerns are key forces behind such changes.

Honesty/Accuracy.   Some would argue that the admissions effort is among the processes most challenged by integrity issues, because it is so influenced by marketing. The institution wants to be presented in the most favorable light, so that prospects will want to enroll. The recruitment process would fail miserably if admissions officials explained all of the problems and weaknesses of the college. However, honest portrayals of the institution can also help prospective students develop reasonable expectations for their college-going experience. This can increase satisfaction and retention, and those results should make consistent candor more important than short-term exaggerations.

This practice relates to the recruitment of athletes. Some prospective students might be told that they have a "good chance" to start at their favorite positions, when there is a returning starter at that spot who was an "all-conference" honoree. This can be unintentional or deliberately misleading, an error at a minimum or fraud at its worst. No matter what, these prospective students are vulnerable to misinformation, and the recruiters should remember that their ethical commitment to candor includes the premise that no information is better than an inaccurate guess.

Orientation is another area where new or transferring students need accurate information about the institution, so that they can develop realistic expectations of their college experience. The program should be balanced in its presentation of aspects of the student experience, presenting the reality of curricular, cocurricular, and extracurricular experiences. Current students can be very useful in this process, adding their voices to those of officials and to the materials published by the institution.

Referrals require as much accuracy and honesty as recruitment. Students can be harmed when staff members treat them beyond their competence or delay them from getting the right help because they were sent to the wrong office. Adequate knowledge and standards should guide student referrals instead of personal hunches.

Confidentiality.   Some professionals understand the importance of student privacy and confidentiality Those who work in student health, psychological counseling, and judicial affairs, for example, are trained about this concern. However, others might be less on the alert about safeguarding students in this way. Family Educational Rights and Privacy Act (FERPA) restrictions are easy to forget, particularly when staff members become aware of information about students that might be compelling or even shocking. Integrity requires adherence and clear guidelines for how information about students is shared inside and outside the university. Individuals might err from time to time, but institutions may not.

Problem Solving.   Some individuals and institutions are better than others at solving problems. Bureaucratic rigidity gets in the way of both. Yielding to traditional authorities can limit the natural problem-solving abilities of people who want to serve current students. This affects many issues that involve the integrity of the institution, and while mistakes are made, the test of integrity is when institutions accept responsibility for their procedures, training processes, or lapsed judgment that created the problems, and address what might need to be changed. No university can have an error-free environment when it comes to how business with students is conducted. However, when what appears to be a problem of integrity arises, a review of the circumstances and responses adds to the perception that the institution has maintained its ethical wholeness and not just its particular structures.

Assessment Possibilities

Responsible administrators need to be alert to clues that integrity might be compromised through its transactions with students. Often, student rates of persistence and graduation demonstrate that there are integrity issues at an institution. Usually, students surveyed at entry reflect a higher expectation of graduation than what turns out to be the case. This does not necessarily mean that students have been duped or that their expectations are unreasonable, but it does suggest that there may be some dissonance between the aspiration of persistence and the reality. Many reasons for persistence problems may exist, and they certainly could include integrity issues that should be addressed in order to enhance the rate of student success (Miller, 2005).

There are different ways to uncover and assess integrity issues. For example, some managers adopt a "secret shopper" strategy, where persons conduct business with a department or organization merely to evaluate its effectiveness and the integrity with which it operates.

A dean of students or campus ombudsman may receive a large number of student complaints about a specific point of student transactions. A pattern of these complaints is certainly worthy of investigation, and addressing their inherent causes is a characteristic of an institution of high integrity.

Any culture with high levels of student complaints and low morale is very important for alert administrators to address. Signals of that culture might include the tone of student government meetings or editorials in the student newspaper. Even the graffiti in the restrooms can be an important indicator of student displeasure. Ascertaining the source or cause of low student morale is essential for student affairs professionals, and determining how to respond is also crucial.

A good sign of perceptions of institutional integrity is an active and engaged student body. Engaged students are happy students. They connect to the programs and services that are designed for their use. Engaging the student community in productive and positive ways does not necessarily mean that there are no integrity issues in the university setting, but it means that those issues are not pushing students away from their involvement with the institution.

Conclusion

Matters of integrity are embedded in many aspects of the campus experience, and administrators need to be alert to how the transactional nature of their work with students affects the structural and ethical wholeness of the institution. Being aware of this fact is an important first step, but responsible student affairs professionals know that they must address and resolve any issues where integrity is compromised.

Bob Young wrote about empirical consistency and coherence in the first chapter, and he made an excellent argument that empirical measures represent consistency and provide a base for fair decision making. What better place to start than consistency and fairness in our dealings with students? These two principles form an excellent foundation for assessing and dealing with integrity challenges.

All the matters that frustrate ethical integrity cannot be erased, but they also cannot be allowed to prevail. Creative, resourceful people find their way around barriers to integrity, and student affairs professionals need to be up to that task. This chapter explored where integrity may be at greatest risk and how those risks might present themselves.

The principles described previously can guide the judgments of student affairs administrators about how to conduct business with students. The transactions that flow from the business relationships with students need to have clarity, consistency, fairness, and participation by students in their design and management.

Under many circumstances, student affairs professionals serve as beacons of integrity, as the institutional community members who respond to crises, and as the ones who manage complicated student problems and help students learn to demonstrate ethical behavior in their daily lives. Those roles cannot be fulfilled effectively unless student affairs professionals display the highest levels of integrity themselves and hold others to the same sort of standards. When we behave in ways that are beyond reproach, then we see issues through the lens of integrity and deal with them in ethically sound ways.

References

Kuh, G. D., Lyons, J., Miller, T. E., & Trow, J. A. *Reasonable expectations*. Washington, DC: National Association of Student Personnel Administrators, 1994.

Miller, T. E. Student persistence and degree attainment. In T. E. Miller, B. E. Bender, and J. H. Schuh (Eds.), *Promoting reasonable expectations*. San Francisco, CA: Jossey-Bass, 2005.

Paine, L. *Cases in leadership, ethics, and organizational integrity.* Chicago, IL: Irwin, 1997.

THOMAS MILLER has been the vice president of student affairs at Eckerd College and Canisius College. He currently holds the position of associate professor in college student affairs at the University of South Florida.

NEW DIRECTIONS FOR STUDENT SERVICES • DOI: 10.1002/ss

5

*Student affairs professionals should value the ideals of
transformational leadership, but they need to navigate the
realities of institutional power structures, if they want to
maintain their political viability and improve
organizational integrity.*

Transformational Leadership, Integrity, and Power

Laura M. Harrison

Transformational leadership enjoys widespread appeal among student affairs professionals. National Association of Student Personnel Administrators (NASPA) and American College Personnel Association (ACPA) conferences frequently feature speakers who promote transformational leadership's two primary tenets: (1) change is the central purpose of leadership, and (2) leadership transcends one's position in an organizational hierarchy. In this chapter, I describe these tenets and analyze their usefulness. I conclude that they are questionable guideposts for many administrators. At the end of the chapter, I offer strategies for dealing with the realities of institutional power.

The Transformational Leadership Dichotomy

The word *transformational* suggests the first tenet of this theory, namely, that affecting change is the central work of leadership. The idea of *management* serves as a contrast. Astin and Astin (2000) argued that:

> Leadership is a process that is ultimately concerned with fostering change. In contrast to the notion of "management," which suggests preservation or maintenance, "leadership" implies a process where there is movement—from wherever we are now to some future place or condition that is different" (p. 8).

Astin and Astin's (2000) distinction between leadership and management mirrors a transformational-transactional leadership dichotomy. The

New Directions for Student Services, no. 135, Fall 2011 © Wiley Periodicals, Inc.
Published online in Wiley Online Library (wileyonlinelibrary.com) • DOI: 10.1002/ss.403

transformational leadership discourse often identifies transactional leadership as its foil. To illustrate, Northouse's (2004) leadership textbook proclaims that:

> Transactional models focus on the exchanges that occur between leaders and their followers [while] ... transformational leadership refers to the process whereby an individual engages with others and creates a connection that raises the level of motivation and morality in both the leader and the follower. This type of leader is attentive to the needs and motives of followers and tries to help followers reach their fullest potential (p.170).

These dichotomies—leadership vs. management and transformational leadership vs. transactional—facilitate an understanding of the concepts at the most basic level. However, portraying leadership as an either-or proposition creates more problems than it solves for student affairs professionals. The management and transactional ends of these dichotomies are the sites where power and politics are acknowledged more openly. By contrasting them to the loftier-seeming notions of transformation and leadership, transaction and management become pejorative labels for essential obligations.

Why, then, does student affairs embrace transformational leadership theory when it fails to address power issues adequately? Love and Estanek (2004) had a concise explanation: "student affairs professionals disdain power as something unsavory" (p. 33). Yet, the very fact that transaction and management recognize systemic power allows them to serve as the vehicles through which transformation and leadership are made possible. Without both an acknowledgment and understanding of how power works in higher education institutions, individual student affairs practitioners are left with a mandate to affect change, but no tools for translating this vision into reality.

Transformational Leadership's Power Problem

Divorcing leadership from positional authority is transformational leadership's second tenet. Proponents of transformational models posit leadership as "quite different from wielding power because it [the leader's agenda] is inseparable from the followers' needs" (Northouse, 2004, p. 170). The notion that "we're all leaders, leading all the time" pervades the transformational leadership literature; supposedly all members of an organization can lead regardless of their place in the hierarchy (Lowney, 2003, p. 15).

This tenet begs the question of what happens when those without positional power attempt to effect change. While some theorists have addressed this subject (for example, Fletcher (2004) and Sinclair (2007)), other widely read authors (to illustrate, Astin and Astin (2000) and Kouzes and Posner (2007)) gloss over the obstacles of confronting organizational power structures. They offer general ideas about leadership, but the specifics of what happens to *this* person trying to effect *this* particular change are ignored in what Badaracco (1997) called the "inspirational ethics literature" of leadership, a genre that hyperbolizes the purity of leaders' motives, their dedication to high aims and noble causes, and their willingness to challenge the system: "At best, these stories provide inspiration and guidance. At worst, they offer greeting card sentimentality in place of realism about why people do what they do" (Badaracco, 2002, p. 35).

In an exhaustive meta-analysis of the literature on leadership in higher education, Kezar (2006) called for more research about power's role in social change. I responded to that call with a study of how student affairs professionals confronted power in institutional change efforts (Harrison, 2010). I interviewed midlevel student affairs professionals from diverse colleges and universities in California and learned that they were labeled troublemakers, passed over for promotions, victims of low morale, and, in the most extreme case, terminated for challenging systemic power in their respective institutions.

My results showed that power structures push back hard against those who challenge them. Parks (2005) reached a similar conclusion in a study of students in leadership classes:

> Nothing was more disturbing to the students as a group than the admittedly provocative suggestion that when they are in a position of formal authority, they have virtually no autonomy. So strong are the forces acting on them to maintain the equilibrium of the social system, they are only puppets on a string (p. 585).

Acknowledging the Realities of Leadership

Leading with integrity requires an acknowledgment of the way power works in organizations. Without such an acknowledgment, potential change agents slip too easily into a hero-martyr mentality, concluding that they must fall on their swords for a cause. Badaracco (2002) warned against such heroic notions. He postulated that much of ethical leadership is about gaining and maintaining access to the table where the day-to-day decisions get made. In other words, sustained leadership comes from insiders who use power and influence responsibly on many issues and over extended periods:

> But people don't become insiders by accident. They must look out for themselves, protect their positions, and stay at the table so they can continue to lead. In other words, they need to have a healthy sense of self-regard. As Machiavelli put it, "A man without a position in society cannot get a dog to bark at him" (p. 35).

This tension between gaining access to power as an insider or challenging the system as an outsider emerged as a consistent theme in my own research. I found that a person could take a stand against an organizational policy or procedure a limited number of times before losing the very position from which he or she could effect positive change. While we are conditioned to think of leaders as those who sacrifice themselves in the service of a greater ideal and there may be situations where this is the necessary and right course of action, it is not a sustainable strategy. Indeed, one of the more alarming findings in my own research was the extent to which the student affairs professionals most committed to principles of social justice were most likely to lose a job, leave the field, or not aspire to higher level positions out of a lack of desire to be an insider within the institution.

Deborah Meyerson (2003) coined the term *tempered radical* to describe the person who can straddle the insider-outsider divide in thinking about organizational change. Tempered radicals "are not heroic leaders of revolutionary change; rather, they are cautious and committed catalysts, ... organizational insiders who contribute and succeed in their jobs. At the same time, they are treated as outsiders because they represent ideals or agendas that are somehow at odds with the dominant culture" (p. 5).

"Ted," a participant in my research, operationalized Badaracco's (2002) and Meyerson's (2003) ideas about the nature of power within the institutional context. He articulated that he achieves success by reading the signals in his organization:

> The VP of Student Affairs never sits down with me and says, "Here are the five things I want you to do this year." I think there are lots of student affairs people who expect that and are bitterly disappointed. I read the university's goals and directions from all kinds of cues, all kinds of things. I find out what the president is saying. I go to all the meetings I can for student affairs managers so I hear what the Vice Chancellor is saying about different programs. I read the newspapers and I know what the university appears to be concerned about. ... So you've got to decipher all of those messages that are both overt and more subtle in terms of how to interpret what direction the university is going in and therefore the role, in my case, the role the residential life system needs to play in that (Harrison, 2006, p. 100).

Similarly, "Ken," another participant in my study, spoke of "taking [his] political temperature" (Harrison, 2006, p. 98) when considering the viability of an advocacy project. Ted and Ken recognized the ways in which power and politics functioned in their respective universities, and were able to enact a transformational leadership vision.

Strategies for Creating More Transformational Systems

Student affairs practitioners can improve their transformational leadership by acknowledging its general limitations, and through the use of specific,

NEW DIRECTIONS FOR STUDENT SERVICES • DOI: 10.1002/ss

systemic strategies to overcome some of the challenges inherent in this model.

Infuse More Political and Business Literature Into Student Affairs Graduate Curricula, Professional Conferences, and Publications. Many in the student affairs profession may shy away from discussions of power, but other professionals do not share their squeamishness. In her book *Bad Leadership*, Kellerman (2004) proclaimed that "the seminal readings in political theory are a treasure trove. Together they provide the single best explanation of why leaders lead and followers follow: self-interest. In nearly every case, leaders and followers engage to protect against the anxiety of disorder and the fear of death" (p. 217). In many universities, individuals and departments vie for dwindling resources, so graduate students and new professionals need to learn about political acumen, hopefully as a component of their professional education.

Corporatization (Bousquet, 2008; Washburn, 2005) characterizes the contemporary university as much as its politics, but the phenomenon is infrequently referenced in the student affairs scholarship and is all but absent from programs at professional conferences. A comprehensive examination of the corporatization literature is beyond the scope of this chapter, but it is worth noting Kezar's (2006) commentary on this trend in higher education: "Research ... demonstrates that campuses are being pressured to centralize power, develop top-down authority structures, cut costs, move away from shared forms of leadership, and adopt corporate management practices, pressures that all run counter to the forms of leadership that are part of the leadership revolution" (p. 150).

Scrutinizing these concerns has led me to conclude that Kezar would advocate the development of business savvy as much as Kellerman (2004) advocated political acumen for effective leadership.

Cultivate Strategic Mentors, Mentees, and Allies. I am conducting ongoing research about the political acumen of student affairs professionals. My participants have expressed strong opinions that graduate programs did not teach them how to negotiate power in university systems, so they have found mentors who give them knowledge and direction when confronted with power issues. Conversely, serving as a mentor renews and increases a leader's knowledge about complex power issues.

Transformational change is rarely, if ever, accomplished without strategic allies in key positions of power. One of my participants told me about a mass e-mail she received from an individual who was trying to unload extra tomato plants from his garden. She said: "Did I want these plants? No. But did I want an excuse to contact him and have him start to know me as a person before I have to pitch a potentially controversial proposal to him next semester? Yes." The plants offered her a chance to find an ally.

Work Through the Public Relations Issues That Affect Student Affairs. The student affairs profession has rarely framed its public image well. The following remarks illustrate the problem (Lewis, 2005):

They [faculty] were, in other words, genuine educational professionals. They left Harvard, or were forced to leave, because they did not fit into the new, retail-store university in which orders are taken, defects are pampered over to get the merchandise out the door, and the customers are sent home happy by "student services professionals" (p. 257).

Such words link student affairs to the corporatization of higher education instead of its transformation. When universities are corporations, students are customers, and student affairs programs are designed to keep the customers happy.

Kirp (2003) seemed to confirm this image, writing about the multiple food options at Babson College: "'It's not about pampering,' insists Carol Hacker, student affairs dean at Babson, all the while maintaining a straight face. 'It's about community building'" (pp. 23–24).

Even though such representations of student affairs cause some degree of discomfort, I argue against dismissing them entirely. Lewis's (2005) and Kirp's (2003) books enjoyed wide audiences, and they shaped, as well as reflected, the thinking of powerful decision makers within colleges and universities. Rather than responding as victims of a false image, student affairs must gain power through providing its own narrative about its operations. Graduate programs, national conferences, and other forums for professional development should help professionals learn how to tell the story of student affairs. If we fail to tell the story of student affairs in a way that is compelling and articulates our clear value, competing entities will frame our work in a way that benefits them, instead of the integrity of the institution. And the students we serve will suffer the consequences.

Reinserting Power Analysis Into Student Affairs' Leadership Discourse

The participants at a recent NASPA Mid-level Professionals Institute received two articles to read before the institute began. The first article was Barr and Keating's (1979) "Establishing Effective Programs." Its authors argued that political savvy was a key student affairs competency, because universities were driven by power structures that must be negotiated in order to advocate successfully for student affairs initiatives. The second article was Allen and Cherrey's (2003) "Student Affairs as Change Agents." Its authors wrote that university structures were not organizational hierarchies, but fluid systems that could be changed by anyone regardless of status. The articles were used to demonstrate the evolution of thought from the political emphasis of Barr and Keating's (1979) older work to the transformational focus of Allen and Cherrey's (2003) newer piece.

Although the presenters juxtaposed these pieces to show a progression from Barr and Keating's (1979) thinking to Allen and Cherrey's (2003) seemingly more enlightened view, I found that the older work resonated

NEW DIRECTIONS FOR STUDENT SERVICES • DOI: 10.1002/ss

more with my own experience as a student affairs practitioner who was try-ing to navigate the realities of university systems. I believed that the earlier literature (Barr and Keating, 1979; Kerr, 1963) articulated a more realistic appraisal of power's role in university leadership. The authors recognized the politics of higher education institutions and, in this acknowledgment, suggested strategies for affecting organizational change.

Ironically, transformational leadership's missing power discourse crip-ples its power to frame and create the kind of change it endorses. As men-tioned in the previous section, teaching and learning how to acquire power through gaining control of the student affairs narrative is one strategy. Aligning change projects with the agendas of power brokers is another. There are numerous ways to attain power in organizations, but the first step requires getting comfortable with power as a tool. It need not be an end, but research and experience suggest power is indeed the means through which student affairs can truly work toward ends, such as the transcendent integrity of the student experience within the corporate institution.

While it might be theoretically true that ethical janitors can be better leaders than amoral presidents, on a day-to-day basis the presidents have exponentially more human and financial resources to implement their visions than a custodial crew will ever have. Transformational leadership tends to minimize some uneven systemic realities or ignore them entirely, leaving students of this theory with a sense of disappointment when they are unable to effect sweeping change from entry level positions within uni-versity power structures. Taking the reality of positional power out of the discourse of leadership limits the accomplishment of the progressive goals of transformative theory that are important to organizational integrity.

It is time for a synthesis that integrates the transformational and trans-actional aspects of leadership and maximizes their benefits. Transforma-tional leadership succeeds in promoting the development of a vision. Divorcing power from position enables members of an organization to identify needs, and in some cases, this softer form of leadership might effect modest change. However, it is insufficient in and of itself for long-term change. On these pages, I have suggested some practical strategies that can create the conditions for transformative change. These strategies empower our purposes. Perhaps ironically, it is through an honest analysis of how power functions in systems that individual student affairs practitio-ners can effect positive change, and feel more positive about themselves, thereby leading with integrity more effectively than ever before.

References

Allen, K., and Cherrey, C. "Student Affairs as Change Agents." *NASPA Journal*, 2003, *40*(2), 29–42.

Astin, A., and Astin, H. *Leadership Reconsidered: Engaging Higher Education in Social Change*. Battle Creek, MI: W.K. Kellogg Foundation, 2000.

Badaracco, J. *Defining Moments: When Managers Must Choose Between Right and Right.* Boston, MA: Harvard Business School Press, 1997.

Badaracco, J. *Leading Quietly: An Unorthodox Guide to Doing the Right Thing.* Boston: Harvard Business School Press, 2002.

Barr, M., and Keating, L. "Establishing Effective Programs." In M. Barr and L. Keating (Eds.), *Establishing Effective Programs. New Directions for Student Services.* San Francisco: Jossey-Bass, 1979.

Bousquet, M. *How the University Works: Higher Education and the Low-wage Nation.* New York: New York University Press, 2008.

Fletcher, J. "The Paradox of Postheroic Leadership: An Essay on Gender, Power, and Transformational Change." *The Leadership Quarterly,* 2004, *15,* 647–661.

Greenfield, T. and Ribbins, P. (Eds.). *Greenfield on Educational Administration: Towards a Humane Science.* New York, New York: Routledge, 1993.

Harrison, L. M. "Advocacy and Agency in Student Affairs." *Dissertation Abstracts International,* 2006, *67*(6). (UMI No. AAT 3221044)

Harrison, L. M. "Consequences and Strategies Student Affairs Professionals Engage in Their Advocacy Roles." *Journal of Student Affairs Research and Practice,* 2010, *47*(2), 197–214.

Kellerman, B. *Bad Leadership.* Cambridge, MA: Harvard Business School Press, 2004.

Kerr, C. *The Uses of the University.* Cambridge, MA: Harvard University Press, 1963.

Kezar, A. J., Carducci, R., and Contreras-McGavin, M. "Rethinking the "L" Word in Higher Education: The Revolution in Research on Leadership." *ASHE Higher Education Report,* 2006, *31*(6).

Kirp, D. *Shakespeare, Einstein, and the Bottom Line: The Marketing of Higher Education.* Cambridge, MA: Harvard University Press, 2003.

Kouzes, J., and Posner, B. *The Leadership Challenge.* San Francisco: Jossey-Bass, 2007.

Lewis, H. *Excellence Without a Soul: Does Liberal Education Have a Future?* New York: Public Affairs, 2005.

Love, P. G., and Estanek, S. M. *Rethinking Student Affairs Practice.* San Francisco: Jossey-Bass, 2004.

Lowney, C. *Heroic Leadership: Best Practices from a 450-year old-Company That Changed the World.* Chicago: Loyola Press, 2003.

Meyerson, D. *Tempered Radicals: How Everyday Leaders Inspire Change at Work.* Boston, MA: Harvard Business School, 2003.

Northouse, P. *Leadership Theory and Practice.* Thousand Oaks, CA: Sage Publications, Inc., 2004.

Parks, S.D. *Leadership Can Be Taught: A Bold Approach for a Complex World.* Boston, MA: Harvard Business School Publishing Company, 2005.

Sinclair, A. "Teaching Leadership Critically to MBAs: Experiences from Heaven and Hell." *Management Learning,* 2007, *38*(4), 458–472.

Washburn, J. *University Inc.: The Corporate Corruption of Higher Education.* New York: Basic Books, 2005.

LAURA M. HARRISON is an assistant professor of higher education and student affairs at Ohio University, and formerly served as the assistant dean and director of the Women's Center at Stanford University.

6

After discussing the relationship between theory and practice, the authors promote assessment as a means to improve the integrity of student development.

Integrity in Student Development

Dennis C. Roberts and Trudy W. Banta

The quest for integrity in practice and theory has been part of the evolution of student personnel work all the way back to the turn of the 20th century. Even our founding philosophical statement, the 1937 "Student Personnel Point of View," could be viewed as an attempt to bring clarity, and thus potential integrity, to our work. Our chapter seeks to take stock of the question of integrity in relation to one of the core knowledge bases used by those engaged in student affairs work today—student development.

We define the key terms we will use at the beginning of this chapter in order to demonstrate the importance of theory to practice work that should be informed by assessment. The next section will describe the historic context for student affairs and how student development came to be one of the primary areas of focus in the 20th century. Based on his administrative experiences, Denny Roberts will explore how theory informs practice and vice versa in resource allocation. Trudy Banta will then explain how assessment has emerged as a central area of concern and focus for demonstrating accountability, and therefore integrity, in both student and academic affairs on the contemporary campus. Her principles of assessment practice will serve as a rubric to determine, at least in this example, whether theory and practice are effectively being utilized to advance assessment work in higher education. In a final reflection, both offer insights on student development and assessment, and their relationship to each other in the current practice of faculty and student affairs staff. This section offers potential accomplishments and challenges as we seek greater integrity in the practice of student affairs.

NEW DIRECTIONS FOR STUDENT SERVICES, no. 135, Fall 2011 © Wiley Periodicals, Inc.
Published online in Wiley Online Library (wileyonlinelibrary.com) • DOI: 10.1002/ss.404

Defining Terms

The first definition of *integrity* in *Webster's New World Dictionary* (1988, p. 702) is "the quality or state of being complete; unbroken condition; wholeness; entirety." This definition captures a portion of our purpose in exploring integrity in student affairs practice. In addition to proposing the ideal that student affairs practice should be complete and whole, another aspect of integrity that many in student affairs would see as important is that the practice and theory would be integrated and consistent. Combining both of these core ideas, integrity in one's work would then involve being fully and holistically informed by theory while seeking purpose and consistency through the interplay of practice and theory.

Student development is both theory based and a goal espoused by many in student affairs. Its roots can be traced to the Progressive Education Movement of the 1920s (Strange, 1994), and it came to fuller maturity in the 1970s. With the advent of the 1970s, student development became synonymous with names such as Sanford, Feldman and Newcomb, Heath, Perry, Kohlberg, and Chickering. Student development can be seen as a reason for being for student affairs, a primary goal of student learning, as well as an information base to enhance the effectiveness of higher education as it helps students achieve more fully informed maturity in the college years.

Assessment involves devising frameworks for learning, determining experiences that potentially contribute to learning, and collecting information of a variety of sorts, which substantiates that learning has occurred or provides information on how progress toward learning and developmental goals might be improved.

The perspective we share here is that the interplay of theory and practice is a necessity in delivering on a commitment to student development. Further, assessment, and subsequent responsive refinement of theory and practice, is a reflection of, and at the core of, integrity in this work.

Emergence of Attention to Student Development (Roberts)

Antecedents of the relevance of student development as a focus for student affairs work can be found as early as the 1920s. Esther Lloyd-Jones (Roberts, 1998) observed that John Dewey's (1923) ideas about democratic education influenced the drafting process that ultimately resulted in the publication in 1937 of the American Council on Education's *Student Personnel Point of View*. Deans of students had begun to appear on some campuses throughout the United States during the late 19th and early 20th centuries. As these deans took on guiding, overseeing, and influencing students' experiences outside class, they sought strategies and philosophical frameworks to bring consistency to their work. The American Council on Education recognized the need to acknowledge this new role in the

NEW DIRECTIONS FOR STUDENT SERVICES • DOI: 10.1002/ss

academy and delegated the task to a writing team that included Lloyd-Jones and ultimately produced the 1937 statement.

Introduction of the idea of student development accompanied the movement to bring coherence to student personnel work. Some authors used the phrase "student development" in titles of publications such as *Student Development: How to Make the Most of College Life* (Walters, 1931) from the very beginning of the field. Student services personnel represented the growing beliefs in collegiate settings that much of learning was occurring outside class and that freeing students to create their own learning while being guided by faculty and staff enhanced all learning. The notion was that by creating a point of view that recognized what was already taking place and then providing ideas or frameworks to deepen that perspective, the growing numbers of students entering colleges and universities and the greater complexity of learning unfolding in those days could be managed more effectively. For the early scholars in student personnel work, the dean's role and the purposes of democratic education espoused by Dewey seemed well aligned to enhance student learning.

The core commitments in the first statement (American Council on Education [ACE], 1937) on student personnel work included preservation, transmission, and enrichment of culture; assisting students in developing to the limits of their potentialities; embracing students as whole beings, including their intellectual capacity, emotional makeup, physical condition, social relationships, vocational aptitudes and skills, moral and religious values, economic resources, and aesthetic appreciation; and exploiting the power of peer interaction in learning. This list defining students' whole being includes the breadth of student development dimensions that remain part of most models even today. The second statement on the purposes of student personnel (ACE, 1949) reinforced much of what was addressed in the first and added that there should be greater emphasis on specialization, efficiency, and productivity. In this statement, which followed World War II, the preservation of democracy was noted as an important commitment as well.

Many student personnel workers of the day assumed that the 1949 statement simply reflected an appropriate refinement of the 1937 statement in this emerging work. However, closer reading reveals a tension between the 1937 statement's admonition that faculty and staff should "regard personnel work as a major concern, involving the cooperative effort of all members of the teaching and administrative staff and the student body" (ACE, 1937, p. 42) and the 1949 statement's adoption of industrial-era perspectives related to bureaucratization, mass production, and clearer administrative organization. Lloyd-Jones and Smith (1954) noted this tension when they reasserted more informal and natural practices in student personnel by saying that "Perhaps their (student personnel workers') most important opportunities are more indirect than direct and exist in their collaborative work with faculty members toward these ends" (p. 12).

NEW DIRECTIONS FOR STUDENT SERVICES • DOI: 10.1002/ss

Despite the warning issued by Lloyd-Jones and Smith and the colleagues who joined them in 1954, the momentum of student personnel work as an administrative area continued, culminating in what was characterized as the student services focus of the 1950s and 1960s. Not until the tumultuous 1970s did other messages about student personnel practice begin to return student personnel to a more educational role. The "Tomorrow's Higher Education" project (Brown, 1972; Miller and Prince, 1977) called for a different kind of student personnel practice, moving away from student service and toward student affairs. These authors and others advocated a return to a more educationally purposeful role for staff who worked in student affairs.

The ebb and flow of perspectives in 1937, 1949, 1954, and the 1970s culminated in the dawning of, and more central role ascribed to, the concept of student development. Knefelkamp, Widick, and Parker (1978) compiled summaries of a number of theories of student development that gave detail, depth, and potential for application to an idea that had been embedded in student personnel work from the beginning. By enlivening the conversation and stimulating the veritable mountain of research and writing that followed, student development became one of the primary theory bases of student affairs work from that time forward. Most of the subsequent models advocated in student learning and deeper engagement rely in one way or another on the student development theories that gained prominence after their advent in the late 1970s.

To come full circle in this brief analysis of how student development has emerged as a central theory base for higher education and student affairs, it is hard to imagine a campus environment being effective in fostering student development if it does not anchor its educational practice at least to some degree in Dewey's (1923) principles of democratic education. A philosophy that involves students actively in their learning is essential if the more specific and refined models advocated in student development research and frameworks are to be effective. And it is hard to imagine a university that is effective in developing students to their fullest potential absent a sense of shared responsibility and investment in achieving this goal across faculty, academic administrators, and student affairs educators/administrators.

Whether in the United States, Europe, Asia, Africa, South America, the Middle East, or elsewhere, student engagement is widely endorsed as adding value to students' higher education experiences. Why? Because theorizing about student engagement, assessment of the student experience, and prevalent student affairs practice have created an ever-improving theoretical framework that has integrity. Even in settings where the national or local government is not democratic in form, student engagement and configuring the classroom to create a more democratic environment are widely advocated.

Student development as a goal, with student engagement as the means to accomplish it, has a very practical challenge—demonstrating that engagement works and discerning the degree to which student affairs programs are contributing to the goal. In very practical terms, while student affairs has experienced amazing expansion over the last century, fiscal and political realities as reflected in today's professional association conference themes/programs and literature make it clear that advocacy for student affairs as a high priority cannot be assumed.

Specific to higher education in the United States, the ebb and flow of the economy, changing demographics, and partisan public officials have produced regular budget reductions and staff retrenchment for decades. The economic recession of 2007–2010 resulted in reductions in workforce and either flat or declining operating budgets at many institutions. While this was under way, it was not uncommon for universities to protect academic programs while demanding disproportionate cuts in student affairs. Depending on the institution, student affairs staff were either asked to "do more with less" or were targeted for reductions that eliminated some functions perceived as nonessential. Student affairs educators have to ask some delicate questions about these reductions. How were the integrity of mission, advocacy for student engagement, purposeful student development design, and assessment of progress examined in making these cuts? Was the loop of design and refinement clear enough and were the outcomes documented in ways to protect those programs that had the best student development outcomes? Or were the decisions based more on opportunity, favoritism, and vested interests? Fortunately, the integrity loop we advocate was observed in many cases. However, some resource allocation decisions were made without consideration of adequate information or the integrity of espoused purpose, student development focus, and data derived from continuous assessment and improvement.

In relation to the emerging international higher education community, the integrity loop is very different. As universities from the United States, United Kingdom, Australia, and other countries expand their presence throughout the developing world, many are simply attending to the academic program with little, if any, attention to student engagement and developmental experiences. In settings where student engagement is at least implicitly sought, two key issues arise—student expectations/preparation and the degree to which personnel in international settings understand and are prepared to deliver student development programs.

On the first question of student expectations/preparation, while high school students educated in the United States are likely to have had some exposure to experiential learning and student empowerment, students in other nations may not have had similar opportunities. When students without experience as engaged learners show up in settings that demand engagement as part of the routine pedagogy in and out of the classroom, there is the potential for a serious disconnect on expectation. At minimum, a period of time will be required for students who are not used to engaging classrooms and out-of-class experiences to adjust to a type of learning that they have not experienced prior to attending a university.

On the second question, the degree to which emerging international universities are prepared to implement student development programs, several questions are yet to be addressed. In many international settings there is little or no understanding of the existence of research, a theory base, literature, and training for student affairs staff. Thus, educators and professional staff from a variety of backgrounds are presumed capable of designing and implementing programs that involve students in their learning and result in the student development outcomes that are advocated in North American models. The problem is that without integrity of theory/practice work that is informed by careful design and assessment of progress, these programs will not benefit from student engagement in the same ways as will those institutions where knowledgeable student affairs professionals are present and active.

In both the United States and internationally, the issue of sustainability has yet to emerge fully. Economic sustainability is not a concern when resources are readily available, the dynamic that was present during the emergence of student development in the 1970s. Economic sustainability has yet to emerge on the international level because higher education outside North America is a growth market. However, the question of sustainability will eventually rise to the surface when expansion stabilizes and tougher resource allocation decisions pit classroom and out-of-classroom learning opportunities against each other.

This example of integrity of practice in resource allocation demonstrates how important it is to make sure that student affairs practice is firmly grounded in educational philosophy, is based on research and theory, and is growing to ward greater integrity of theory and practice aimed at achieving student development outcomes. How to apply assessment so that it provides the evidence that student affairs professionals and other educators need is the topic to which we now turn.

Linking the Ideal of Theory With Practice.   As we seek to influence student development, we are often thrown into situations or dilemmas that require balancing the generality and idealism of theory with the reality of practice. In a very simplistic way, theory stimulates us to ask critical questions while proficiency in practice provides tools that allow us to be competent and effective. Having questions without tools to respond only frustrates us. If we have not asked the right questions, even effective practice could fail because it does not respond to the appropriate question or concern. The fusion of theory and practice then provides the opportunity to address the best questions and adapt the most effective responses to them. This fusion is impossible without active use of data derived from assessment.

Assessment—An Example of Theory and Practice (Banta)

Emphasis on collaboration among colleagues is a hallmark of my work. I encourage faculty to work together across disciplines and student affairs professionals to share with each other what they are learning in their various divisions. In addition, I believe it is essential that faculty and student affairs professionals work as partners in enhancing student learning. Another important collaboration is between theorists and practitioners throughout higher education.

In this world of instant communication and rapid change, those of us who are administrators must make dozens of decisions, often about very different matters, every day. Student development theory is one source of information we can use to inform our judgments, but many decisions must be made so quickly that most often we must rely on intuition, past experience, and knowledge of the immediate context to shape our thinking. When we have the privilege of a bit more time to reflect before making a decision—as we do when planning to invest in a long-term strategy to promote student success and persistence—we should look for assistance from our colleagues who study and develop theory. When I have time to think, one of the many examples I can read is a chapter about psychosocial, cognitive structural, and person-environment interaction theories written by Kuh and colleagues (2002). If one or more of those theories informs my work and I can demonstrate that the outcomes of my practice either strengthen the theory or call some aspect of it into question, then I think we have a good blend of theory and practice, or integrity in theory and practice.

Because our lives are so hectic, and decisions must be made so quickly, many college and university administrators are relieved when they find simple lists of principles based on research that they can apply in their work. The sets of principles I have in mind are not usually based on a single theory but rather on multiple field tests of a variety of theories. In fact, they are often called "principles of good practice," not theory per se.

One such listing that has shaped thinking among faculty and student affairs professionals alike is the Wingspread Seven Principles for Good Practice in Undergraduate Education (Chickering & Gamson, 1987). These principles, based on the findings of many theory-based research projects, were intended to advise decision makers that college students' learning would be enhanced if they experienced opportunities for interaction with faculty on intellectual matters outside class, collaboration with other students on academic projects, active learning, assessment of their performance and assignments with prompt feedback, time on task, high expectations, and respect for diverse talents and ways of learning. These principles clearly suggest many opportunities for academic and student affairs collaboration to further student learning. At hundreds of institutions the principles have been used to guide initiatives intended to promote learning and persistence to graduation. And while at most institutions we are far from completely successful in attaining our goals for student development, research has continued to demonstrate the efficacy of employing these principles in a variety of settings. In 2005, Kuh, Kinzie, Schuh, Whitt, and Associates published the results of research involving 20 institutions that have higher than predicted retention and graduation rates and reaffirmed that student success is promoted by setting high expectations for learning; assessing learning and using the results both to inform students of their strengths and weaknesses and to discern the kinds of changes in instruction that are needed to enhance learning; and using engaging pedagogies such as active learning, group activities based on collaboration among peers, and approaches that embody respect for a variety of learning styles.

My own field of outcomes assessment in higher education is highly interdisciplinary in its foundations. Scholars interested in theories of learning, student development, organizational development, and cultural change, as well as program evaluation and measurement, have contributed to the assessment literature. Thus, no assessment theory has emerged independent of these antecedent fields. But we certainly have developed our share of principles of good practice! I have one of my own that I began working on two decades ago (Banta, 1993). I published another version in 2002, confirmed many of its components in a 2005 study (Banta & Lefebvre, 2006) that involved interviews with 11 college and university presidents and vice presidents, and used a second slightly modified version to organize 49 examples of good practice in a more recent book (Banta, Jones, & Black, 2009). Over the years, my set of principles has benefited from the work of others on similar lists, including Hutchings (1993); American Productivity and Quality Center (1998); and Jones, Voorhees, and Paulson (2001). In the paragraphs that follow, I sketch my principles, or characteristics of effective assessment as I have called them, and illustrate them with comments drawn from the interviews conducted in 2005 (Banta & Lefebvre, 2006).

The top administrators interviewed in spring 2005 included four current or emeritus presidents, six chief academic officers, and a chief student affairs officer. They represented two- and four-year, public and private, colleges and universities located on campuses across the country. These individuals were chosen because their institutions have been recognized in the literature by assessment practitioners as models of good practice.

When I asked the interviewees if their work had been shaped by a particular theory, not one said "yes." Thomas Corts, then president of Samford University in Alabama, summed up the prevailing sentiment most succinctly: "I'm not really interested in those theories." Nevertheless, most described their leadership styles as collaborative. Austin Doherty, vice president emeritus of Alverno College in Milwaukee, said, "leadership is really collaborating . . . facilitating collaboration . . . engaging in teamwork."

I view assessment as a three-stage process. Thus, the characteristics of assessment practice on my list are grouped in three sections based on whether they occur in the planning, implementing, or improving/sustaining stage of assessment.

Planning.   The first characteristic in the planning phase of effective assessment is that stakeholders—faculty, administrators, students, student affairs professionals, and community representatives—are appropriately involved so as to incorporate their needs and expectations in the plan for assessment and ensure their later support. Earl Lazerson, president emeritus of Southern Illinois University Edwardsville, asserted, "You can have all the transformation vision in the world, and if you don't have a sufficient cohort of people to buy into that," the vision will never be realized.

A second planning characteristic is the *development of clear, specific, program objectives* as part of a plan with purposes that are related to goals stakeholders value. Effective assessment is not a process to be undertaken for its own sake, without connection to other important programs and processes. When a new approach to general education or a new student activity is being planned, an ideal opportunity to connect assessment to each of the program goals exists. Charles McClain, president emeritus at Northeast Missouri (now Truman) State University, believes that assessment can be "a really powerful force for change . . . a great tool for improving instruction." Karen Bowyer, president at Dyersburg (TN) State Community College, views assessment as "a way to improve the quality of services and student learning . . . a way to be a much better institution."

Implementation.   In the implementation phase of assessment, the first characteristic is *knowledgeable, effective leadership*, both from the president and chief academic and student affairs officers and from faculty or staff members who are given the day-to-day responsibility for institutional effectiveness activities campus-wide. Charles Schroeder, former vice president for student affairs at the University of Missouri–Columbia, practices a leadership style that asks colleagues to set "stretch goals," aiming a bit higher than they think they can go. Schroeder believes "a lot of progress occurs when you're willing to look not at the way things are, but at how they can be and how we can get there."

In implementing assessment successfully, there should be widespread recognition that *assessment is essential to learning and therefore is everyone's responsibility*. We recognize that most of students' time is spent outside the classroom. Thus, student affairs professionals must be important partners with faculty in extending learning and assessment to that substantial component of time when students are not in class.

Successful assessment implementation includes *faculty and staff development*—preferably together—to prepare individuals to implement assessment and use its findings. According to Douglas Brown, then provost at James Madison University in Virginia, "the ability of faculty (and staff) to participate in assessment varies widely," so "for the last 20 years we have been training faculty (and staff) . . . how to build assessment into their curricula."

William Miller, then provost at the U.S. Naval Academy, said, "The most effective initiatives are those that the faculty (and staff) own. I try to get down to the grassroots and stimulate growth rather that directing programs."

Successful assessment *devolves responsibility for assessment to the unit level.* When assessment findings are presented, faculty and staff need to see the results of their own work reflected in unit-specific data wherever possible.

Successful assessment recognizes that *learning is multidimensional and developmental and thus incorporates multiple measures* to maximize reliability and validity, thereby establishing credibility for its methods and findings. A student studying organizational leadership may demonstrate knowledge of the characteristics of a good leader through high scores on classroom tests, but having the assessment of a student affairs professional who has observed the student in the process of bringing about change in a campus organization adds credibility to the evaluation of the student's leadership capacity.

Successful assessment is *undertaken in an environment that is receptive, supportive, and enabling*—on a continuing basis. Not only is faculty and staff development provided as needs are identified, but faculty and staff are recognized and rewarded for assessing their work and making warranted improvements. Margaret Malmberg, previously the provost at the University of Charleston in West Virginia, believes that "moving the assessment agenda . . . is about changing a culture," and "the more time and energy and resource you put into it, the greater the risk. The risk is high . . . but there's also substantial gain." "Building trust and relationships is all important" in implementing assessment, observes Michael Durrer, emeritus vice president for instruction at Mt. Hood Community College in Oregon. Both Miller and Malmberg discussed methods for recognizing assessment efforts in reward structures. At the Naval Academy, assessment is recognized "as a part of teaching in awarding merit pay increases," Miller reports. Malmberg adds, "We have embedded assessment as part of our annual review process for faculty and staff, for promotion and retention, for merit pay."

Successful assessment *incorporates continuous communication with constituents concerning activities and findings.* It produces data that provide direction for continuous improvement of programs and services. Tom Corts recognizes the need "to keep everybody informed." He asserted, "We've done everything from mass meetings to small group meetings and different in-between levels to try and be sure people understand what we're talking about."

Improvement.   In its third phase, assessment must produce improvements and be sustained. Effective assessment ensures that *assessment findings are used continuously to improve programs and services.* Jack Lohmann, then vice provost at Georgia Tech, demonstrates why outcomes assessment plays an important role at his institution when he states, "We're driven by data." Brown adds, "Data determine what we fund." Durrer believes that faculty and student affairs staff will use data if they see that "dollars are available to help improve programs, especially those that really need improvement."

Successful assessment provides a means of *demonstrating accountability to stakeholders* within and outside the institution. Assessment yields data for performance indicators that gauge progress toward institutional and unit goals, and the performance indicators (macro indicators) can be used in reports for both internal and external audiences. For instance, at the University of Missouri, the provost asked about learning communities, "What difference do they make and why should I pay anything [for them]?" Schroeder collected longitudinal data that demonstrated positive relationships between participation in a learning community and both learning gains in general education and retention to graduation (the six-year graduation rate climbed from 58 percent to 66 percent during Schroeder's tenure). The data convinced the provost to commit funds for additional learning communities.

Successful outcomes assessment *incorporates the expectation that it will be ongoing, not episodic*. Faculty and staff often ignore initiatives they regard as temporary. Therefore, an assessment culture must be sustained over the years, as it has been since 1970 at Alverno College and Truman State and since 1985 at James Madison University. As Corts put it, at Samford, assessment is "an expectation—just the way we do business."

Successful assessment *incorporates ongoing evaluation and improvement of the assessment process itself*. Like every other component of an institution, assessment processes must be evaluated for effectiveness annually according to objectives set locally, and every 5 to 10 years by an external body. The form of evaluation will be directed by local and regional, or national, norms. Some institutions bring in external reviewers to assess campus programs and services every 5 to 8 years. Others may rely on decennial visits of teams sponsored by regional accreditors to provide evaluation of the assessment function. No assessment process is working so perfectly that some suggestions for improvement by outside observers will not be warranted.

While not guided by theory per se, the foregoing characteristics of successful outcomes assessment are based on years of field tests of concepts based both on theory and practice. The iterative process of hypothesizing, testing in practice, theorizing, and then hypothesizing, testing, and theorizing again forms the basis of integrity in student affairs.

Concluding Reflections—Integrity of Student Development and Assessment

We propose that, indeed, the iterative process of using student development theory to inform practice and the interplay of student development with assessment processes can and should bring greater integrity to student affairs work. The question is the degree to which this mutually informing dynamic regularly unfolds.

Both of us are actively engaged in translating student development theory in our respective work. Perhaps the greatest explicit and deep use of theory is seen in the design and early implementation of new initiatives. These are the result of task force work, consensus building, and collaborative staff initiatives. Sometimes planning is stimulated by crisis. We hope that conscientious planning is more often the result of reflecting on the information we gather and seeking to improve effectiveness by fine-tuning our programs through the use of this information.

The practical world of student affairs administration requires that multiple influences be considered. Budgetary restraints, political implications, and the availability of qualified and effective personnel are just three of the influences that must be factored into most decision making. However, these are intervening influencers in contrast to student learning outcomes. On the grander level, student learning and development have to be the ultimate outcomes we seek. If student learning and development are not the transcending outcomes on which we are focused, most of our institutional mission statements will need to be rewritten.

What are the conversations like when decision making is under way? Are they about resources and difficult relationships, or are they about the outcomes we anticipate for students? Even when organization structure is an important and necessary consideration, are the people involved in the structure the most important component, or is it the potential improvement in program quality and the benefit to students that are paramount? These and other questions must be pondered as we attempt to assess the degree of integrity we achieve in student development work.

We propose that considerable improvement in applying theory in our practice is possible and necessary if higher education is to achieve more fully the level of effectiveness that students, families, employers, communities, public authorities, and others are beginning to expect of us. In order to stimulate enhancements currently advocated (Keeling, 2004), data analyses should be undertaken to determine the degree to which funding and facilities allocations in higher education are consistent with mission and goals statements. We propose that analysis of institutional decision-making processes should be undertaken and that this information should be used to discern the focus and rationale for our decisions. We propose that the degree of fit between graduate preparation in student affairs and the work competencies required of young professionals also be investigated. And we advocate that midcareer and senior staff in student affairs reflect on their purposes and the roles they play in shaping their institutions' agenda for student learning. The ongoing concerns of student affairs staff are driven by many issues. However, a consistent keynote and workshop theme at our annual meetings calls all of us to look at ourselves, the complex environments in which we work, and the potential we have to create greater integrity in our work as educators. These questions are salient and concrete and they are more than relevant to our future welfare as student affairs practitioners.

References

American Council on Education. *The Student Personnel Point of View.* American Council on Education Studies, Series 1 (Vol. 1, No. 3). Washington, DC: Author, 1937.

American Council on Education, Committee on Student Personnel Work. *The Student Personnel Point of View* (rev. ed). American Council on Education Studies, Series 6, No. 13. Washington, DC: Author, 1949.

American Productivity and Quality Center. *Benchmarking Best Practices in Assessing Learning Outcomes: Final Report.* Houston, TX: Author, 1998.

Banta, T. W. "Characteristics of Effective Outcomes Assessment: Foundations and Examples." In T. W. Banta and Associates. *Building a Scholarship of Assessment.* San Francisco: Jossey-Bass, 2002.

Banta, T. W. "Summary and Conclusion: Are We Making a Difference?" In T. W. Banta and Associates. *Making a Difference: Outcomes of a Decade of Assessment in Higher Education.* San Francisco: Jossey-Bass, 1993.

Banta, T. W., Jones, E. A., and Black, K. E. *Designing Effective Assessment: Principles and Profiles of Good Practice.* San Francisco: Jossey-Bass, 2009.

Banta, T. W. and Lefebvre, L. A. "Leading Change through Assessment." *Effective Practices for Academic Leaders,* 1(2). Sterling, VA: Stylus, 2006.

Brown, R. D. *Tomorrow's Higher Education: A Return to the Academy.* Student Personnel Series No. 16. Washington, DC: American Personnel and Guidance Association, 1972.

Chickering, A. and Gamson, Z. "Seven Principles for Good Practice in Undergraduate Education." *Wingspread Journal,* 1987, 9(2), 1–4.

Dewey, J. *Democracy and Education.* New York: Macmillan, 1923.

Hutchings, P. "Principles of Good Practice for Assessing Student Learning." *Assessment Update,* 1993, 5(1), 6–7.

Jones, E. A., Voorhees, R. A., and Paulson, K. *Defining and Assessing Learning: Exploring Competence-based Initiatives: A Report of the National Postsecondary Cooperative.* Washington, DC: U.S. Department of Education, National Center for Education Statistics, 2001.

Keeling, R. P. (ed.). *Learning Reconsidered: A Campus-wide Focus on the Student Experience.* Washington, DC: National Association of Student Personnel Administrators and the American College Personnel Association, 2004.

Knefelkamp, L. L., Widick, C., and Parker, C. A. (eds.). *Applying New Developmental Findings. New Directions for Student Services,* no. 4. San Francisco: Jossey-Bass, 1978.

Kuh, G. D., Gonyea, R. M., and Rodriguez, D. P. "The Scholarly Assessment of Student Development." In T. W. Banta and Associates, *Building a Scholarship of Assessment.* San Francisco: Jossey-Bass, 2002.

Kuh, G. D., Kinzie, J., Schuh, J. H., Whitt, E. J., and Associates. *Student Success in College—Creating Conditions That Matter.* San Francisco: Jossey-Bass, 2005.

Lloyd-Jones, E. M., and Smith, M.R. *Student Personnel as Deeper Teaching.* New York: Harper, 1954.

Miller, T. K., and Prince, J. S. *The Future of Student Affairs.* San Francisco: Jossey-Bass, 1977.

Roberts, D. C. "Student Learning Was Always Supposed to Be the Core of Our Work—What Happened?" *About Campus,* 1998, July/August, 18–22.

Strange, C. "Student Development: The Evolution and Status of an Essential Idea." *Journal of College Student Development,* 1994, 35, 399–412.

Walters, J. E. *Student Development: How to Make the Most of College Life.* New York: Pitman, 1931.

Webster's New World Dictionary: Third edition. New York: Simon and Schuster, Inc. 1988.

DENNIS C. ROBERTS *is an assistant vice president for Faculty & Student Services at the Qatar Foundation in Doha, Qatar.* TRUDY W. BANTA *is a professor of higher education and senior advisor to the chancellor for academic planning and evaluation at Indiana University–Purdue University Indianapolis.*

7

The purpose of this chapter is to examine the conceptual frameworks and strategies that can be used to teach graduate students and new professionals how, when, and where to lead with integrity.

Teaching Integrity

Sue Saunders and Jennifer Lease Butts

Integrity is one of those essential yet highly ambiguous concepts. Although no definition can perfectly communicate the intricacies and subtleties inherent in the term integrity, the following definition communicates the essential essence of the concept. For the purpose of this chapter, integrity is defined as that combination of both attributes and actions that makes entities appear to be whole and ethical, as well as consistent.

We know integrity when we see it, and perhaps we recognize the concept even more profoundly when it is absent. Like the concepts of leadership or wisdom or community or collaboration, integrity is a key element of effective practice in student affairs administration. Yet one cannot teach integrity simply by subdividing the concept into discrete components and communicating or debating the particular elements. Integrity is best learned through reflective practice in an environment that requires one to resolve complex problems with deliberate attention to their moral and ethical implications.

As stated earlier in this volume, infusing one's identity and administrative practice with integrity encompasses more than the straightforward application of ethical standards or virtues. Operating with integrity certainly relies on congruence with ethical principles and virtues, but it extends further—to include an ability to analyze a problem of practice, to design a resolution, to summon the moral courage to actually enact the solution, and perhaps most importantly, to make midcourse corrections in light of multiple contexts and emerging self-understanding. Integrity incorporates the consistency and coherence of our actions, the complexity of our analyses, and the ability to empathize with others, as well as the clear understanding of our own virtues and deficits (Chapter 1).

New Directions for Student Services, no. 135, Fall 2011 © Wiley Periodicals, Inc.
Published online in Wiley Online Library (wileyonlinelibrary.com) • DOI: 10.1002/ss.405

Leading with integrity is complex because most often student affairs professionals don't have the luxury of choosing one or two easily identifiable courses of action. As Kidder (1995) pointed out, most complex choices are not simple dilemmas with two potential solutions, one right and the other wrong. Instead, student affairs professionals can encounter tri lemmas, dilemmas with a middle ground (Kidder, 1995), or ethical problems with many feasible solutions. Whether one, two, or more alternatives seem to be available, no administrator can ever be certain that a chosen course will lead to positive outcomes, no matter how pure one's intentions.

Current Contexts That Make Integrity Important to Learn

A quarter century ago, Brown (1985) argued that the common mission of student affairs professionals was to be the moral conscience of the college campus. He believed that student affairs professionals must support high standards of ethical conduct, and he added that professionals must confront all who fail to meet these standards. In essence, Brown challenged professionals to become campus leaders of integrity.

Student affairs administration in the mid-1980s was arguably simpler than it is in the 21st century. To maintain integrity today, student affairs professionals have to work with students who differ from their predecessors. In addition, they have to contend with fewer resources, more legal risks, and the commercialization of higher education.

Today's students have been exposed to situations and opportunities that do not foster ethical integrity as much as they violate it. To illustrate, the incidence and sophistication of academic cheating have risen dramatically since the 1980s. New information sharing technologies and new opportunities, such as custom essay writing companies, make plagiarism easier than ever. Recent research (Lloyd, Dean, & Cooper, 2007) posited that Facebook and related networking technologies may have a negative effect on developing healthy peer relationships that deepen empathy, altruism, and other social virtues that are essential to integrity.

Many universities are trying to save resources by outsourcing services to third party vendors who provide everything from assessment consultation to residence life training to student success coaching. How can student affairs administrators deal with these cuts in staff and resources, and still design campus systems and processes that are internally coherent and provide consistent outcomes?

They have to try. It is doubtful that vendors will sustain the relationships, educational perspectives, and commitment to institutional culture (Lipka, 2010) that are identified with the structural integrity of student affairs. Yet the degree of that integrity communicates powerful lessons to undergraduate students, graduate students, and new professionals who are looking for student affairs to act in accord with its espoused values of quality and service.

NEW DIRECTIONS FOR STUDENT SERVICES • DOI: 10.1002/ss

The ever-increasing legal implications of professional practice challenge the structural and ethical integrity of student affairs. Some professionals and institutions try to avoid legal risks through avoiding them, and that inhibits operating in a consistent, coherent, virtuous, and empathic way (Winston & Saunders, 1998). For example, a campus recreation professional might try to avoid legal risk by eliminating club sports. The risk is stronger than the ethical imperative to benefit students.

Effective student affairs professionals operate in a legally prudent manner that maintains the integrity of their practice (Bickel & Lake, 1999). However, this type of skillful professional practice requires vigilance in understanding the law as well as careful reflection about what action is most congruent with professional virtues and principles.

The commercialization of higher education creates additional integrity lapses within the higher education enterprise (Bok, 2003). Almost every week another scandal comes to light, such as: a university's effort to gain a larger market share of individual or corporate largesse; illegal athletic recruiting (Suggs, 2004); the influence of corporate sponsorship on research (Basken, 2009), or the deceptive marketing of student loans and alleged payoffs to several university financial aid officers. These and other scandals undermine public confidence in higher education. Aspiring, new, and established student affairs professionals are not immune from public skepticism about their universities' capacity to operate with integrity.

Teaching Integrity: Beginning With Frameworks

In *The Courage to Teach*, Parker Palmer (1998) stated that good teaching comes not from a particular technique, but from weaving one's identity and integrity into one's practice, so that techniques "reveal rather than conceal the personhood from which good teaching comes" (p. 24). Knowledge of self and of contexts is integral to the process.

While new institutional and societal forces affect student affairs, its administrative context is inherently filled with ethical and structural dilemmas. Student affairs administrators need well-honed skills to deal with them. Some of these dilemmas are posed in a comprehensive book of case studies that was generated by seasoned and new professionals (Hamrick & Benjamin, 2009). They challenge anyone's assumptions that it is simple to solve issues such as: the equitable treatment of students, fairness in position searches, impact of those influential in institutional politics, misuse of alcohol, and diversity commitments. Careful analysis is needed in order to resolve these types of dilemmas with any degree of coherence, consistency, and morality. That analysis should begin with reflection about ethical principles, moral virtues, and personal beliefs.

External Frameworks.   Two frameworks can help administrators analyze ethical dilemmas: (1) professional standards and their foundational principles, and (2) moral virtues. Unfortunately, professional standards are rarely straightforward. Scholars from a variety of disciplines have offered multiple and conflicting sets of them. Couple the multiplicity of advice they offer with an administrator's tacit beliefs about what is right and wrong (Hamrick & Benjamin, 2009; Nash, 2002), and it becomes clear that any professional needs to reflect extensively before making initial judgments about a dilemma. Experience and support from communities and mentors will help. Then the administrator needs to challenge assumptions and take risks in order to act intentionally and consistently on her judgments.

Ethical Standards and Principles. Since the early 1980s (Winston & McCaffrey [Saunders], 1981), student affairs professional associations have developed and revised ethical standards statements. Ethical standards are essentially sets of rules derived from agreement among professionals that guide professional conduct (Winston & Saunders, 1991). Often, these rules reflect broader principles. For example, Kitchener (1985) developed a commonly used set of principles that includes the injunctions to benefit others, promote justice, respect autonomy, be faithful, and do no harm. When the ethical rules are silent on a particular issue, the underlying principles can provide some guidance.

Two "umbrella" student affairs associations, the American College Personnel Association (ACPA, 2006) and the National Association of Student Personnel Administrators (NASPA, 1990) have published ethical standards to guide student affairs professionals. Although these standards are generally congruent with each other, the ACPA standards focus on responsibilities to students and the NASPA standards emphasize responsibilities to colleges or universities.

Recently, ACPA and NASPA (2010) have identified professional competencies, and practicing with ethical integrity requires: (1) articulating a personal code of ethics based on professional association standards, (2) knowledge of these standards and their foundational principles, and (3) the ability to analyze. The knowledge of professional standards is a good place to start, but not sufficient by itself. Hamrick and Benjamin (2009) stated:

> If professional standards or formal statements were prescriptive and absolute sources of guidance in ethically problematic situations, no ethical decision making would be required of professionals—other than the choice to consult the appropriate statement and follow the directive (p. 7).

The guidance of ethical standards contributes to the "reflective" part of practicing with integrity; the "practice" component must be supplemented by the will to act with structural and ethical integrity. This will to act is often a component of individual character and more aligned with the moral virtues view of ethical integrity.

Moral Virtues. Moral virtues offer a more flexible framework for guiding the development of ethical integrity. Virtues are those characteristics of particular people in particular contexts that are considered good or right within that context (Fried, 1997). Fried identified four virtues that are commonly deemed worthwhile for student affairs professionals: *prudence*, being thoughtful and unwilling to jump to conclusions; *integrity*, demonstrating behavioral consistency from one situation to another; *respectfulness*, thinking through responses to others; and *benevolence*, considering others' well-being. These virtues have been incorporated into the *ACPA Statement of Ethical Principles and Standards* (ACPA, 2006).

Virtues describe the character of the person seeking to operate with integrity, instead of the rules and consequences in standards and principles. Virtues focus on "who should I be" rather than on "what should I do." The framework of virtues assumes that ideal traits lead to the common good and individual development within a particular context. In our case, student affairs administrators who have these virtues are self-reflective, operate transparently, and examine the consequences of their behavior.

Individual Beliefs.   Ethical standards and ideal virtues provide external frameworks that can influence professional integrity. They are necessarily limited, since a significant portion of their content has been derived from the beliefs of the dominant culture. Fried (1997) pointed out the limits of relying on concepts of "good" and "right" that are embedded in "common life experience and worldview related to race, socioeconomic status, professional identity, gender, sexual orientation, or disability" (p. 6).

External frameworks are less accessible than those internal values and worldviews that come from an individual's experience, cultural traditions, or simply temperament. These background beliefs (Nash, 2002) are powerful, tacit influences on the way in which a given professional practices. Therefore, "reflection, acceptance of differences, and increased self-knowledge can help . . . professionals consider the ways in which aspects of the individual backgrounds inform their perspectives, their working assumptions about the world, and what they value" (Hamrick & Benjamin, 2009, p. 9).

Activating Reflection

Learning how to think carefully about ethical principles, moral virtues, and personal beliefs is the first step toward practicing with integrity. The multi-dimensional nature of student affairs work requires additional steps, and these steps involve action and reflection after action.

How do we move content and context into practice without simply throwing graduate students and new professionals into the deep end of the pool? What methods can we use to teach them to work intentionally across their experiences and reason their way through an integrity dilemma? These questions can begin to be addressed by considering the following elements as we teach integrity: the locations where we teach, the teaching philosophy we employ, the methods we use, and the relationships we have with those we are teaching.

NEW DIRECTIONS FOR STUDENT SERVICES • DOI: 10.1002/ss

Teaching Locations

When thinking of graduate students, the classroom seems the obvious and easy answer to the question of location for teaching integrity. Most preparation programs offer classes in law and ethics, and so it might seem natural to think that integrity is taught there and move on to other matters. Doing so, however, diminishes the breadth and depth of learning for our graduate students. Our educational system subdivides courses and concepts, and this makes the synthesis of concepts across courses much more difficult for students. When a complex concept like integrity is kept inside one course on law and ethics, our students lose the chance to see its implications in other classroom contexts. Discussions about integrity and examples of integrity dilemmas need to take place across our curriculum.

The classroom is a natural and appropriate setting for discussing integrity frameworks and contexts, but it should not be the only setting that we employ. By using professional practice as a teaching location, new professionals are able to investigate the integrity dilemmas of practice, adding to the benefit for all concerned. Integrity can become an integral learning construct in acculturation, new staff orientation, and the supervision of graduate students and new professionals.

Acculturation is the process of familiarizing a person with the culture of a particular environment. It is an important part of the development and socialization for new professionals and graduate students (Tull, Hirt, & Saunders, 2009). There are many cultural environments to discover in a student affairs position. For example, a new professional needs to learn about the cultures of students, offices, departments, the division, and the institution, and then relate that knowledge to the larger cultures of the student affairs profession, higher education, states, regions, and nations. Cultures are continually evolving, so acculturation is a continuing concern of integrity. When integrity and acculturation are linked through conceptual discussions and real dilemmas, graduate students learn how to improve practice and their own transitions to new positions and institutions.

Orientation is the process by which a department trains new staff, sets expectations, and begins the acculturation process for new professionals (Winston & Creamer, 1997). It presents another opportunity for teaching about integrity. Current staff can model behaviors and demonstrate leadership when they show new staff how they work through ethical dilemmas. In turn, new staff will develop ethical reasoning skills and gain important insights by watching and listening to their colleagues (Blimling, 1998). Using real-world dilemmas boosts the quality of learning in the orientation process (Saunders & Cooper, 2009).

Supervision offers new professionals the opportunity to engage in deep, reflective conversations one-on-one with a more experienced colleague. These conversations can be structured to engage new professionals in the multifaceted challenges of integrity. A recent study revealed that experienced student affairs professionals found new role models when leaders and mentors discussed ethical reasoning with them (Reybold, Halx, & Jimenez, 2008). Role models are critically important to the acculturation of all professionals, including new staff and graduate students.

Teaching Philosophies

Successful teachers have philosophies that fit with their personal beliefs and interests (Palmer, 1998). However, the ability to fit teaching philosophies to the subject matter might ultimately shape our ability to teach integrity with integrity.

Creating a shared philosophy for teaching and learning may be one of the most important steps. Baxter Magolda (1992) uses three teaching principles—validating the learner's knowledge, situating learning in the learner's experience, and mutually constructing meaning—to create a learning partnership, and to spur self-authorship "by modeling it and providing participants the kind of support they needed to shift from external to internal self-determination" (Baxter Magolda, 2004, p. 43). The pedagogies we use to teach integrity can profit from these principles. They help create the knowledge, skills, and beliefs necessary for graduate students and new professionals to act accordingly and on their own when faced with professional dilemmas.

Rest's (1994) model of morality is another helpful framework. Its four components are moral sensitivity, moral judgments, moral motivation, and moral character. They apply to, a process for moral decision-making, including understanding context, determining what ought to be done, balancing competing values, and developing the psychological ability to act. Guthrie (1997) described some of the benefits for using this model to teach integrity when she wrote: "Rest's model shows how the pieces fit together and provides a framework for understanding what it takes to succeed in performing a moral act (or, conversely, the different reasons why a person might fail to behave morally" (p. 33).

Teaching Methods

It is important to have discussions about integrity in different locations, and the methods that we use to engage in these discussions are equally important. Kolb's (1981) research on learning styles provides a framework for understanding the different ways people learn and develop. He suggested different teaching methods to reach and challenge all learning styles. We believe that graduate students and new professionals can benefit from in-depth discussions, experiential learning, and case studies about integrity dilemmas.

In-depth discussions offer time to unpack the "areas of gray" around integrity dilemmas. Grappling with issues of right versus right and how professionals make decisions in these dilemmas may be easier for new professionals and graduate students to accomplish in groups. The groups can be facilitated through active reflection, guided discussion, and perspective taking to advance their understanding (Saunders & Cooper, 2009). A classroom example of these approaches might be to ask groups of students to take opposing perspectives and discuss whether new professionals should be Facebook friends with their students. Groups could be asked to make a decision by creating a personal policy statement on the issue after listening to both sides.

Experiential learning yields opportunities to apply knowledge and to learn from hands-on involvement with material. Experiential learning methods include role-plays, participant-observation activities, and skill-training exercises (Johnson & Johnson, 2009). Johnson and Johnson (2009) described several of the benefits of these activities:

1. People believe in knowledge they discover.
2. Active learning is more effective than passive learning.
3. Groups are more effective than individual attempts to change beliefs and theories.

The application of experiential learning to teaching integrity could benefit from a cognitive apprenticeship approach, which employs observation, debriefing, and coaching as a multistep process of active learning for a graduate student or new professional (Saunders & Cooper, 2009). Learners could observe an experienced professional verbally reasoning through an integrity dilemma. The experienced professional could then debrief the decision making process with the learners, and then give a group of learners additional dilemmas to process aloud for further debriefing. This process could be repeated several times so that sustained coaching can occur and ensure deep, active learning on the part of the graduate students or new professionals.

Finally, case studies provide a means of combining in-depth discussion with hands-on experiential learning. Case study analysis uses details and common contexts to provide a structure for discussion and problem solving (McKeachie, 2002). Graduate students and new professionals can apply theories to practice in a controlled environment. Some case studies are created by teachers, but others can be drawn from current events in higher education, providing an immediacy and a relevancy for students. Graduate students and new professionals may have more patience when wrestling with difficult concepts like integrity dilemmas if the need for this analysis is apparent in the headlines of the day.

Experiential learning and a case study approach could both be used in staff training to teach graduate students and new professionals about integrity in supervision. Learners could be presented with the integrity dilemma of wanting to supervise student staff in a way that is fair and equal and also in a way that meets students' developmental needs. The developmental differences between students should allow for a "right versus right" scenario where a supervisor must grapple with how to provide individual and development supervision to students and simultaneously supervise in a manner that is fair and equal—and appears fair and equal—to all of the student staff members. The strength of these teaching approaches lies in creating real-life, timely dilemmas that graduate students and new professionals actively confront in a safe environment with a trusted and resourceful teacher. As a result, the relationship of teacher to learner is worthy of consideration.

Teaching Relationships

The final and perhaps most critical element for teaching integrity is building relationships with graduate students and new professionals. Mentoring and role modeling have been part of student affairs practice since long before it was labeled "student affairs" practice. Winston and Hirt (2003) wrote that mentors and supervisors have to provide role modeling and counseling to new professionals. Integrity at its core asks individuals to consider who they want to be as professionals, and who can better help them answer that question than a trusted mentor and role model.

Even in the absence of mentoring relationships, conditions can be created that promote the trust needed to learn and explore concepts of integrity. First, we can create safe spaces and fill them with safe professionals. This means establishing an atmosphere where it is safe to question, seek help, and make mistakes. Safe professionals might be people other than one's supervisor or faculty advisor who can be turned to when a new professional is faced with a dilemma. Even the most caring and supportive supervisors and faculty members cannot eradicate the power differential in their relationships with supervisees or students. They can, though, help identify other colleagues and trusted professionals to serve as resources for students.

Conclusion

Teaching integrity is intertwined with integrity-laden professional practice. If we want graduate students and new professionals to gain deep learning about integrity, they need to see similar behavior and hear similar messages from a variety of professionals in a variety of contexts. Both faculty and practitioners need to be engaged in deep reflection about standards, virtues, and personal guidelines of integrity; they need to talk about ethical dilemmas, and they need to be clear, consistent, and transparent in their decision making. Then they will be role models who are engaged in a mutual process of learning with younger professionals. Learning from each other and making this shared learning habitual may be the best way to face our current integrity dilemmas, preparing all of us to face the unknown ones we shall have to face in our future.

References

American College Personnel Association: College Student Educators International. *Statement of Ethical Principles and Standards.* Washington, DC: Author, 2006.

American College Personnel Association: College Student Educators International and National Association of Student Personnel Administrators. *Professional Competency Areas for Student Affairs Practitioners.* Washington, DC: Authors, 2010.

Basken, P. "Science Rules Leave Room for Scandals." *Chronicle of Higher Education,* 2009, July 20. Retrieved from http://chronicle.com/article/Science-Ethics-Rules-Leave/47083/

Baxter Magolda, M. B. *Knowing and Reasoning in College: Gender-related Patterns in Students' Intellectual Development.* San Francisco, CA: Jossey-Bass, 1992.

Baxter Magolda, M. B. "Learning Partnerships Model." In M. B. Baxter Magolda and P. M. King (eds.), *Learning Partnerships: Theory and Models of Practice to Educate for Self-authorship.* Sterling, VA: Stylus, 2004.

Bickel, R., and Lake, P. *The Rights and Responsibilities of the Modern University: Who Assumes the Risk of College Life?* Durham, NC: Carolina Academic Press, 1999.

Blimling, G. S. "Navigating the Changing Climate of Moral and Ethical Issues in Student Affairs." In D. L. Cooper and J. M. Lancaster (eds.), *New Directions for Student Services,* No. 82. *Beyond law and policy: Reaffirming the Role of Student Affairs* (pp. 65–75). San Francisco, CA: Jossey-Bass, 1998.

Bok, D. *Universities in the Marketplace.* Princeton, NJ: Princeton University Press, 2003.

Brown, R. D. "Creating an Ethical Community. In H. D. Canon and R. D. Brown, *Applied Ethics in Student Services.* San Francisco, CA: Jossey-Bass, 1985.

Fried, J. "Changing Ethical Frameworks for a Multicultural World." In J. Fried (ed.), *New Perspectives on Education, Student Development, and Institutional Management.* New Directions for Student Services, No. 77. San Francisco, CA: Jossey-Bass, 1997.

Guthrie, V. L. "Cognitive Foundations of Ethical Development." In J. Fried (ed.), *New Perspectives on Education, Student Development, and Institutional Management.* New Directions for Student Services, No. 77. San Francisco, CA: Jossey Bass, 1997.

Hamrick, F. A., and Benjamin, M. *Maybe I Should: Case Studies on Ethics for Student Affairs Professionals.* Lanham, MD: University Press of America, 2009.

Johnson, D. W., and Johnson, F. P. *Joining Together: Group Theory and Group Skills* (10th ed.). Upper Saddle River, NJ: Pearson, 2009.

Kidder, R. M. *How Good People Make Tough Choices.* New York, NY: Harper Collins, 1995.

Kitchener, K. "Ethical Principles and Ethical Decisions in Student Affairs." In H. J. Canon & R. D. Brown (Eds.), *Applied Ethics in Student Affairs. New Directions for Student Services,* No. 30. San Francisco, CA: Jossey-Bass, 1985.

Kolb, D. A. "Learning Styles and Disciplinary Differences". In A. W. Chickering & Associates, *The modern American college: Responding to the New Realities of Diverse Students and a Changing Society.* San Francisco, CA: Jossey-Bass, 1981.

Lipka, S. (2010, June 13). Student Services, in Outside Hands. *Chronicle of Higher Education.* Retrieved from http://chronicle.com/article/Student-Services-in-Outside/65908/

Lloyd, J., Dean, L. A., and Cooper, D. "Students' Technology Use and Its Effects on Peer Relationships, Academic Involvement, and Healthy Lifestyles." *NASPA Journal,* 2007 44(3), 48–56.

McKeachie, W. J. "Problem Based Learning: Teaching with Cases, Simulations, and Games." In W. J. McKeachie (ed.), *Teaching Tips: Strategies, Research, and Theory for College and University Teachers.* Boston: Houghton Mifflin Company, 2002.

Nash, R. "Real World" Ethics: Frameworks for Educators and Human Services Professionals (2nd ed.). New York, NY: Teachers College Press, 2002.

National Association of Student Personnel Administrators. *NASPA Standards of Professional Practice.* Washington, DC: Author, 1990.

Palmer, P. J. *The Courage to Teach: Exploring the Inner Landscape of A Teacher's Life.* San Francisco, CA: Jossey-Bass, 1998.

Rest, J. R., & Narvaez, D. (eds.). *Moral Development in the Professions: Psychology and Applied Ethics.* Hillsdale, NJ: Erlbaum, 1994.

Reybold, L. E., Halx, M. D., & Jimenez, A. L. "Professional Integrity in Higher Education: A Study of Administrative Staff Ethics in Student Affairs." *Journal of College Student Development,* 2008, 49(2), 110–124.

Saunders, S. A., and Cooper, D. L. "Orientation in the Socialization Process." In A. T. Tull, J. B. Hirt, and S. A. Saunders (eds.), *Becoming Socialized in Student Affairs Administration.* Sterling, VA: Stylus, 2009.

Suggs, W. "Lawmakers Hear NCAA Plans to Reform Recruiting and Academics." *Chronicle of Higher Education,* 2004, May 28. Retrieved from http://chronicle.com/article/Lawmakers-Hear-NCAA-Plans-to/28476/

Tull, A. T., Hirt, J. B., and Saunders, S. A. *Becoming Socialized in Student Affairs Administration.* Sterling, VA: Stylus, 2009.

Winston, R. B., and Creamer, D. G. *Improving Staffing Practices in Student Affairs.* San Francisco, CA: Jossey-Bass, 1997.

Winston, R. B., and Hirt, J. B. "Activating Synergistic Supervision Approaches: Practical Suggestions." In S. M. Janosik, D. G. Creamer, J. B. Hirt, R. B. Winston, S. A. Saunders, and D. L. Cooper (eds.), *Supervising New Professionals in Student Affairs: A Guide for Practitioners.* New York: Brunner-Routledge, 2003.

Winston, R. B., and McCaffrey (Saunders), S. A. Development of ACPA Ethical and Professional Standards." *Journal of College Student Personnel,* 1981, 22, 183–189.

Winston, R. B., Jr., & Saunders, S. A. "Professional Ethics in A Risky World." In D. L. Cooper & J. M. Lancaster (eds.), *Beyond Law and Policy: Reaffirming the Role of Student Affairs.* New Directions for Student Services, No. 82. San Francisco, CA: Jossey Bass, 1998.

Winston, R. B., Jr., & Saunders, S. A. "Ethical Professional Practice in Student Affairs." In T. K. Miller & R. B. Winston, Jr. (eds), *Administration and Leadership in Student Affairs: Actualizing Student Development in Higher Education* (2nd ed.). Muncie, IN: Accelerated Development, 1991.

SUE SAUNDERS *is an extension professor of higher education and coordinator of the higher education and student affairs master's program (HESA) at the University of Connecticut.* JENNIFER LEASE BUTTS *has been a teacher and administrator in higher education for 15 years, and is currently an associate extension professor in the University of Connecticut HESA program.*

8

The author interviewed six leaders about challenges to their professional integrity. The themes from those interviews are offered in this chapter.

Give In or Get Out? Responding to Professional Challenges

Robert B. Young

A master's student weaved through the crowd at a reception and reached me with a big frown on his face and an equally big question on his mind. He had been invited to interview for a position at a conservative institution and wondered aloud: "What if I do what I think is right, and I'm fired because it (angers) my boss?"

I remembered something as I struggled for an answer. Several years earlier, Frances Lucas provided the keynote at a midlevel managers conference. She started off with three words: "Save your money." Money in the bank could preserve their integrity on the job. It is easier to speak truth to power when a person's financial security is not endangered.

I realized that this counsel would not ease my student's fears, nor would my second thought—"Well, it happens"—but other resources were at hand. Several leaders in our field were at the reception, and I introduced my student to two of them. After the introductions, I mentioned that this leader had been fired for his integrity, and that vice president quit a job because of hers. Then I added that I could have introduced this student to many others in our profession: men and women who left or lost their jobs when their integrity was at stake. Most of them would (as I was told during my research for this chapter) "rather live on a bench and suck a rock" than sacrifice their values for the sake of any job.

In this chapter, I offer some themes that emerged from a set of conversations that I had with six student affairs leaders. I hoped to construct a small case study about challenges to the integrity of student affairs leaders from those conversations. As with any qualitative case study, the purpose was to generate hypotheses rather than to test them.

New Directions for Student Services, no. 135, Fall 2011 © Wiley Periodicals, Inc.
Published online in Wiley Online Library (wileyonlinelibrary.com) • DOI: 10.1002/ss.406

I promised my respondents that I would cloak their identities as thoroughly as possible in this chapter because integrity challenges are noisy and notorious, and their effects seem to linger forever. I wanted to protect my respondents from any unpleasant echoes, so some gender, location, and other identifying aspects of the stories have been changed in this presentation.

The protocol was straightforward. I asked each person a series of questions that fit a chronology of crisis: the background and context of the incident, the way that the respondent analyzed the dynamics and professional impact of the incident, and its short-term and long-term consequences. The conversations were recorded, and basic content analysis was conducted to identify and categorize any themes.

Inevitability

The stories confirmed my long-standing opinion that integrity conflicts are inevitable in student affairs administration. We deal with complex ethical issues, and perspectives about them can be in conflict with each other. Not necessarily because one perspective is wrong and another is right, but because one type of right is in conflict with a different type of right (Kidder, 1996). Truth can conflict with loyalty, individual rights with community responsibilities, short-term results with long-term consequences, and justice with mercy for mistakes.

Our primary professional interest is the overall learning environment and the learners within it, instead of other interests such as institutional stability or academic continuity. Vice presidents of finance, chairs of boards, and academic vice presidents have top priorities that conflict with ours. They are not wrong when they disagree with us, just differently right. Empathy can help us understand each other, but it cannot prevent conflicts when the moral and material interests of any institution are at odds with each other.

Scott Rickard and Linda Clement (1991) studied successful administrators for their book, *Effective Leadership in Student Services*. They determined that student affairs leaders can "work to avert crises . . . [but they] . . . also accept their inevitability" (p. 145). Rickard and Clement described several environmental, protest, international, and policy crises that give "leaders the opportunity to assume a role that is natural to them, and one that fulfills their own need to assist others—on a larger scale" (p. 164). They concluded that student affairs leaders relish this role.

Integrity and Student Affairs Leadership

In addition, Rickard and Clement determined that student affairs leaders possess three primary attributes: (1) *integrity*, involving trust, honesty, loyalty, courage, and risk taking; (2) *commitment*, evidenced by a positive attitude toward students, enthusiasm, joy, and passion for the work; and (3) *tenacity*, focusing on hard work, patience, and follow-through. Integrity is first and foremost.

Eleven years later, Thomas (2002) concurred with Rickard and Clement. He wrote that, "At its core, student affairs leadership centers around ethical values, integrity, and the courage to do the right thing at the right time" (p. 61).

Integrity is far more important than longevity, as William Butler asserted in *Effective Leadership* (Rickard & Clement, 1991):

> To survive over the years as a senior administrator in several major universi-
> ties is by no means an easy task. To survive nearly forty years in administra-
> tion with perceived integrity (among) one's colleagues and others is a far
> greater accomplishment (p. 20).

My respondents would agree with that, and they would add that their integrity was doubted or feared more than it was understood at the time of their crises. For example, one respondent was walking through a reception line the day that he lost his job, and one of the greeters (another cabinet officer) left the line abruptly to avoid shaking hands with him. My respondent wondered if he was carrying an infectious disease on his hand, something that could rub off and terminate the job of anyone who shook it.

Types of Challenges

The leaders faced an array of challenges involving athletics, academic discipline, cultural identity, institutional image, personal attributes, policy, residence life, and state politics. Their challengers were trustees, presidents, politicians, and students. Although all my respondents were current or past vice presidents, only one talked about a challenge that came from a member of her staff.

The Themes

Four basic themes emerged from my conversations. They involved identification challenges, loyalty conflicts, faith, and the healing power of integrity. Those themes have a loose association with chronology and a tighter one with each other. Identification challenges partnered with loyalty conflicts. Faith supported my respondents through the conflicts and helped them heal afterward.

Identification Challenges.   One respondent has been challenged about her regional and institutional understanding throughout her career. She wanted the readers of this chapter to "realize how vulnerable they are" to people who consider them to be outsiders at the places where they work. This vice president felt that she was always an outsider at one institution

NEW DIRECTIONS FOR STUDENT SERVICES • DOI: 10.1002/ss

we talked about. Her gender and background limited her acceptance and, therefore, her effectiveness inside the institution.

Cultural Identification.   One of her challenges could have been titled "you gotta know the territory," a line from a song in *The Music Man*. The singers predict that Harold Hill will never sell a trombone in Iowa because he is an outsider. He does not know how the residents of River City go about their business.

Another respondent said that he thought he knew his territory, the South, until he worked at an institution deep within the region. His integrity was challenged right away, and suspicions or direct distortions of his work followed him every day he was there.

"It all began innocently." He was put in charge of an upcoming funding campaign. The campaign was supposed to be secret in order to protect potential donors, but rumors developed that the campaign was designed to destroy the Old South traditions of the institution. My respondent received an anonymous e-mail from Europe, which was followed by phone calls, death threats, and plain-clothes police protection for him and his family. The president and board did not give him permission to reveal the inside facts of the campaign until after the Ku Klux Klan rallied on campus.

Identification With Prior Administrations.   Overidentification with an institution can be equally challenging. Presidential leadership changed during two vice presidents' terms, and even though they thought they had outlasted challenges to their integrity, they lost their jobs because they were identified with the preceding administration.

Personal Identification.   Students and staff raised different questions about the insider–outsider status of two vice presidents. In one of the cases, lesbian, gay, bisexual, or transgender (LGBT) members confronted an openly gay vice president in his office. They wanted him to advocate for LGBT issues on campus and off, in person and through different media. The vice president's career and personal life had suffered from oppression because of his identity, but he told the students that he was the vice president for all of the students, and not just for groups he had historical connections to. He added that the president and the board knew his orientation, so he was not closeted. It was no secret to anyone. It was not his sole standard for dealing with issues of equity and justice, either. He was going to serve all of the students all of the time and judge the merits of any situation one at a time.

Loyalty Conflicts.   Identification challenges were intertwined with conflicting demands on the loyalty of my respondents: to their institutions, to prior administrations, to staff or superiors, and to students.

Institutional Conflicts.   Two respondents said that their crises involved a basic choice. They could be true to the long-standing values of their institutions or to its short-term realities. My respondents chose the values, while their presidents and board members chose the realities. These power brokers wanted to protect reputations and resources that were in jeopardy if the vice presidents had their way.

Reputations and Resources.   The issues stemmed from judiciary decisions about basketball players. While the misconduct of football players is well known, the consequences are greater for basketball teams. Only 12 students, rather than 80, need to be in uniform for games, and one or two star basketball players can move small, as well as large, institutions into national prominence very quickly. When this happens, the institution's reputation increases and so do its financial rewards from television and tournament appearances. The road to fame and fortune is more cost-effective on the court than on the gridiron, at least until the star players leave before graduation, are injured, or get into trouble. The team's entire season can be ruined when that happens, so a decision about student discipline can turn into a career-threatening challenge for the decision maker, the vice president of student affairs.

I learned that outside forces had pressured student judicial boards to make lenient decisions about basketball players at both institutions. The vice presidents overturned the decisions despite their exposure to similar pressures. Afterward, one of the vice presidents walked into the president's conference room for a meeting and found the National Collegiate Athletic Association (NCAA) procedural officer and a lawyer, the president and university counsel, and the chair of the board of trustees already seated. An empty chair was waiting for her. The coach had threatened to resign, and the president and the chair of the board wanted to hold onto the fame and the fortune that his teams brought to the institution. The others were there to show her how.

After surveying the surroundings and wondering, "Where is *my* lawyer?" the vice president defended the rationale behind the judiciary process, told the others that it could not be manipulated, and asked, "Do we (meaning the university as a whole) stand for what we say we believe [in regard to academic standards]?" The penalties were postponed until the basketball season was over, and then the vice president was advised to "get with the picture" by some trustees, ordered to attend a make-up meeting with the basketball coach, and eased out of her position a year later. The basketball player went to the NBA.

The other vice president suspended key members of the basketball team for sexual assault, because the evidence was against the players even if students, the president, some trustees, and the local newspapers wanted to keep them on the court. The president fired my respondent, and he was prevented from taking a subsequent position until all the legal issues were settled. He told me, "It was simple; they did it," and relied on religious faith to get through the days, weeks, and years after his decision.

In both institutions, one large and one small, the presidents valued the success of their basketball teams more than the student conduct system. The vice presidents were charged with disloyalty to their institutions when they upheld truth over the political and economic consequences of their decisions. The vice presidents thought that they were being loyal, not disloyal, to their institutions, since they were upholding purposes and processes that were proclaimed in handbooks and other media.

Loyalty to Prior Administrations.   I noted earlier that several of my respondents went through presidential changes during their integrity crises. They liked many of the old and new holders of that position, and they tried to be loyal, so long as they remained there, to each person who steered the institution. The change in top leadership did nothing to improve their situations, however, in part because the boards of trustees that hired the new presidents did not change membership. One vice president thought he would have been eased out of the institution even if no incident had happened, because loyalty to an outgoing president does not guarantee any sort of tenure with a new president.

Loyalty to Staff.   One vice president learned that "perception is everything" when he decided to explore extended visitation hours in the residence halls on his campus. He decided to run a pilot program in two single-sex halls, and gained approval but no formal vote from the board for it. My respondent told campus news about the test program, and this small item turned into a lead story in the largest paper in the state. "Sleepovers With Opposite Sex" was the headline. He dropped the pilot study and prepared a statement about his decisions. The president told him to blame a new, junior staff member for the brouhaha, but he would not. He took full responsibility and never spoke casually or assumed approval of his actions at the university again.

Loyalty to Students.   One vice president was new to her campus, so she attended the meetings of each student group at the start of her first academic year. Some members of the university community assumed that she would advocate for ethnic diversity because she was a person of color and her personal beliefs were well known. Other underrepresented groups demanded special treatment, because she was "one of them." They did not care that she had just joined the administration, or that her objective was to assess the dynamics on campus before making any promises to any group. She told students, "If I say I'm going to do something, I will do it," but not until she examined the situation for herself.

The advisor for the Queer Student Coalition did not accept that. When she met with his group, she told the members that she hoped to get resources and full-time staff support for them, but the advisor wanted a commitment for those resources then and there, as well as a promise to resign in two years if she did not deliver. Without those commitments, he accused, she would be another disappointment; she would mean nothing more to LGBT students than any other establishment insider. My respondent asked for a chance to learn the system. She told him to check with her former employer about her character, but otherwise "I don't roll like that." She sat with the staff member after the meeting and asked why he stayed in a place that he thought was so toxic. "Well, economic times are hard," and squirmed through all the reasons why he had to hold on to his job and why

NEW DIRECTIONS FOR STUDENT SERVICES • DOI: 10.1002/ss

it was such a miserable job. She told him, "I would rather sit on a bench and suck on a rock than let a place get me down like that."

Faith

My respondents were supported by religious faith, the faith of their families, and their faith in the profession. Two of them are deeply religious people. One is guided by the humble belief that God's plan is perfect and he has a place within it, no matter how things are going for him at any particular moment. The other told me that she stops to remember the most important fact about her work when it is easy to "go the other way": "I am a steward of everything. My job is to make sure that the Owner is happy."

Religious faith helped these two respondents, while another tapped his faith in his family to get through the challenges. The love of his partner, the needs of his children, and loving memories of his father helped sustain his integrity.

All my respondents talked about their faith in the deep purposes of their work. I heard repeated expressions that they had to be "true to the students." I do not believe that they had any particular students in mind, but rather, they had to be faithful to the value of what it means to be a student and what it takes to serve them with integrity. Other loyalties did not matter as much. Loyalty to the culture, to one's supervisor, or to the espoused mission of the institution would all lead to a change in their employment. What's left? Loyalty to the truth they found in the values of the field.

The Healing Power of Integrity

Rickard and Clement (1991) wrote that student affairs leaders relish challenges, but I did not talk with anyone who enjoyed these challenges to their integrity. They valued the experiences in retrospect, however. Crisis affirmed their grit, even though they suffered material and psychological consequences from it: "I had to accept what happened. It was hard to change roles."

I might have abetted this conclusion by intentionally selecting the people I talked with. They were of different ages, ethnicities, and orientations, but I focused on people who faced challenges to their integrity and came through the challenges with their values intact.

It had nothing to do with *how* these few people made the case for integrity, nor that they thought it was their only alternative. One said that he inherited his father's values, and he could not let his father down. Another said, "I could have gone along. I could have toed the party line . . . but no, I couldn't." In the midst of crisis, all of them found out, as Mark Twain admonished, that their foremost obligation, at any time, was to do what they believed was right.

The other unanimous conclusion was that they became better professionals because they maintained their integrity. When they realized that they did not "know the territory" in which they worked, they shored up their assessment skills. Political savvy was developed, including new approaches to communication. The "recovering extrovert" learned that he had to "choose words more carefully." Another learned to separate what she could control from what she could not: "If it doesn't kill me, it makes me wiser, a better person, and a better supervisor because it's not about me." To these leaders, the crisis required one way of dealing with a situation and learning several skills from it.

Generating Hypotheses About Integrity Challenges

In other chapters, the following might be offered as suggestions for practice. Here, and in keeping with case study research, the suggestions are offered as hypotheses that need to be tested.

- Integrity challenges are inevitable due to the complexity of student affairs issues and transitions of personnel.
- Student affairs leaders will be challenged by perceptions that identify them as institutional insiders or outsiders.
- These perceptions are affected by stereotypes within and beyond the institution.
- Intuitive assessments of institutional culture must be checked continuously.
- Identification challenges are connected to loyalty challenges.
- Leaders should remain loyal to the values of the profession when their loyalty to institutions or administrations is challenged.
- Leaders should assert their advocacy for all students even if their loyalty to some students is challenged.
- Honesty is essential to a leader's integrity, and prudence should guide its expression.
- Faith sustains a leader through a crisis regardless of the short-term consequences.
- Maintaining integrity leads to long-term satisfaction and skills development.

Conclusion: The Heroes' Adventures

Joseph Campbell (1956) wrote *The Hero With a Thousand Faces,* an analysis of mythological heroes who ventured through the wilderness. This chapter was an analysis of the adventures of six vice presidents into and beyond some challenges to their integrity. My respondents do not consider themselves heroic, but they fit Campbell's description of heroes. They are trustworthy people who represent an ideal. These attributes resonated through my respondents' tales about the challenges they faced, the actions they took, the mistakes they made, the lessons they learned, and the self-confidence they enjoy from keeping their integrity intact.

Their stories are historical but not exclusive. As one of my respondents declared, all student affairs administrators need to "realize how vulnerable they are" to challenges to the integrity of their own practice. They will have opportunities to test the hypotheses that these leaders have generated through their stories.

References

Campbell, J. *The Hero with a Thousand Faces.* New York: Meridian Books, 1956.
Kidder, R. *How Good People Make Tough Choices: Resolving the Dilemmas of Ethical Living.* New York: Simon and Schuster, 1996.
Rickard, S., and Clement, L. *Effective Leadership in Student Services.* San Francisco: Jossey-Bass, 1991.
Thomas,W. "Moral Domain of Student Affairs Leadership." In J. Dalton and M. McClinton (eds.), *The Art and Practical Wisdom of Student Affairs Leadership. New Directions for Student Services,* no. 98. San Francisco: Jossey-Bass, 2002.

ROBERT B. YOUNG is a professor of higher education and student affairs (HESA) in the Patton College of Education and Human Services at Ohio University.

9

Hurricane Katrina displaced 400,000 residents along the coast of the Mississippi, and destroyed hundreds of thousands of homes and businesses across Mississippi, Louisiana, Alabama, and Tennessee. This chapter examines the preparation and response of one college's senior leadership team to the disaster and to the needs of students, families, and the surrounding communities.

Gone With the Wind? Integrity and Hurricane Katrina

Frances Lucas, Brit Katz

The unthinkable happened. Hurricane Katrina slammed into 80 miles of Mississippi shoreline on August 29, 2005. It was the nation's worst natural disaster, a perfect storm. One hundred sixty miles-per-hour winds sent 55-foot-tall waves and a 30-foot wall of water across the shore and miles inland. The storm displaced 400,000 residents of the region. However, the damage did not stop there. Flooded rivers, gorged bayous, and tornadoes took their toll beyond the borders of Mississippi.

Millsaps College is located 160 miles north of the Gulf Coast, in the state's capital of Jackson, Mississippi. It is a nationally prominent residential liberal arts college with a renowned history in the Civil Rights movement of the 1950s and 1960s. Twelve hundred student-scholars were enrolled at the college on the day the hurricane unleashed its wrath.

The days leading to the hurricane's impact were ominous. The president and the college emergency management team began reviewing meteorological reports and National Oceanic and Aeronautical Administration forecasts. The entire campus shifted into emergency preparedness mode, with a plan focused on safety, security, and consistent communication. President Lucas said, "It's coming and it's the real thing; it's a Category Five."

The staff presumed (accurately) that power would be interrupted; therefore, the communication plan was developed to operate with or without electricity. Regular time and space were created for the community to meet for the latest news.

Three days prior to the storm, the president canceled all classes until further notice. Students were encouraged to leave campus and find even

NEW DIRECTIONS FOR STUDENT SERVICES, no. 135, Fall 2011 © Wiley Periodicals, Inc.
Published online in Wiley Online Library (wileyonlinelibrary.com) • DOI: 10.1002/ss.407

safer shelter from the storm. Nonetheless, many students traveled toward the Gulf of Mexico to help prepare their homes for the impending disaster. Other students chose to remain on campus, so decisions had to be made on where to locate students during the worst parts of the storm.

Staff inventoried flashlights, portable generators, water, food, gasoline, and batteries. Computing technicians suspected a loss of power and related challenges, so the mainframe computer was deactivated hours before the storm to better protect the system and its software from potential damages.

Messages were sent to parents and other family members who lived in areas that were supposed to be hit by the storm. The messages invited them to stay in the residence halls at Millsaps College with their students. Many staff decided to remain on campus, sleeping in lounges and offices, on couches and floors, awaiting the storm's onslaught. College Chaplain Lisa Garvin said, "I decided to stay on campus, because I live (nearby) in a little house surrounded by trees. And I felt safer being in these sturdy buildings."

The Campus Community

Storm-level winds arrived around 1 P.M. on the fateful day of impact. Tornado sirens emitted their screams. Power lines were ripped from their connections, and within a few hours, the campus was darkened along with most of the Jackson-Metro area. Only 3 percent of city residences and buildings had power immediately after the storm trampled the city. Century-old trees fell across formerly manicured campus lawns. Roofs were punctured, and some were blown away. Centralized heating and air conditioning systems were rendered inoperable. The storm inflicted $1 million of estimated damages on a campus that was three-plus hours away from the coast.

A few cell phones operated, but most cell phone users were unable to contact family and friends on the Gulf Coast, in New Orleans, or in storm-blasted regions. Patti Page Wade, the college director of marketing and communications, said, "As cell phone service became patchy or nonexistent, and as media outlets that did have working land lines were inundated with calls, we used fax and even hand delivery of messages to the media."

The community's misery levels were compounded by the inability to satisfy personal needs. Most electricity lines were downed, and the city's water treatment facility was inoperable without electricity. On campus, toilets could not be flushed, people could not take showers, and potable water became increasingly scarce.

A devoted group of housing resident assistants went in search of drinking water. They were forced to travel to the Mississippi Delta region, more than two hours northwest of campus, to find stores with bottled water for sale.

Since gasoline stations depended on electricity to power their pumps, the loss of utilities created an unexpected fuel shortage. Some supplies were

NEW DIRECTIONS FOR STUDENT SERVICES • DOI: 10.1002/ss

temporarily available in cities with electricity, so employees traveled to Vicksburg, Mississippi, 45 miles west of campus, to purchase gasoline. However, these supplies were short-lived, and gasoline soon became scarce across the entire Southeast region of the nation because supply lines were impaired by the storm.

Intangible psychological concerns went hand in hand with the tangible ones. Students, families, and college employees were grief-stricken about their losses, and fear-stricken about the unknown. The college chaplain's office provided centralized grief counseling stations so that community members could air their feelings about issues and seek relief. For example, many students and employees were unaware of the fate of their families on the Gulf Coast or in New Orleans. Even though administrators discouraged students from returning home for reasons of safety, some anxious and frightened students announced their intentions to drive home anyway. As a result, administrators nervously helped these students prepare for what had been warned as a dangerous journey to the coast.

Conversely, many family members of the affected students moved onto the Millsaps campus immediately after the hurricane, despite the outages of electricity, water, and gasoline. The college conditions were far from ideal for the families, but hotels in the region were overflowing with refugees, and any roof over one's head was welcomed respite.

The Local Community

It was quickly evident that city managers could not immediately stabilize utilities and services, so the president consulted with available members of the college emergency management team, made a careful assessment of the situation, and decided to close the campus for two weeks. The hiatus was supposed to give the campus and local community enough time to regain equilibrium. However, resources from national relief efforts—usually available during emergencies such as Katrina—did not materialize in some areas until much later, so the community did not stabilize as desired. Millionaires and low-income citizens were still sharing desperate life circumstances. Since national relief was unavailable, local religious groups organized, and outside volunteers swarmed into the area, escorting blessed supplies, staffing, and hope to a blighted area.

Millsaps students volunteered to assist many community agencies. Some helped staff the regional Red Cross effort; conveniently, the Red Cross offices are situated one city block from our campus, which was an easy walking distance for students who were suddenly without cars.

Other students helped recalibrate computers at various metro offices. Varsity athletes helped unload planes transporting relief supplies. And some students helped displaced people at various churches and at a regional shelter housed at the Mississippi Coliseum, the designated site for refugees from the disaster.

NEW DIRECTIONS FOR STUDENT SERVICES • DOI: 10.1002/ss

Restoring the Campus Community

Administrators estimated that 164 current students awoke the day after the storm to find many important resources gone. Either they lost their homes or their parents no longer had any place to work. Few colleges could absorb the costs of helping current students, and Millsaps was no different. The chair of the board of trustees and the president asked for and accrued $3 million from donors and foundations to support the overall recovery and response mission. Since federal aid was made available for hurricane-affected students, the director of financial aid applied for, and Millsaps was rewarded with, $4 million in direct aid for students.

However, federal aid was unavailable for campus restoration projects, so dedicated faculty, staff, and students decided to return to campus to clear debris, remove fallen trees, collect rubbish, and repair roiled landscaping. The maintenance staff constituted one of many teams that remained on campus throughout the storm period, and they joined students to form a "bucket brigade" that brought water from the campus swimming pool to replenish and flush campus toilets. Dining services professionals cooked by candlelight and gaslight to provide nutrition; social fraternities volunteered their services to the kitchen staff for preparing meals.

Serving Displaced Students.   The immediate travails of the greater New Orleans metropolitan area were well documented in the media, but few people outside the region know about a diaspora of college students from the affected city center to college and university campuses across the South and elsewhere. Millsaps admissions officers opened their suites and welcomed applicants who had to transfer from the hardest hit institutions in the city. The college enrolled at least 60 undergraduates from those institutions, including students from Tulane University, Dillard University, the University of New Orleans, and Delgado Community College. There were no enrollment records or transcripts for these students, so the admissions officers had to trust them to provide proper information. In addition, many of these students appeared on campus with nothing more than the clothes on their bodies and a small backpack. Other college officials assisted them with obtaining clothing, food, toiletries, bedding, and supplies.

Maintaining Institutional Integrity

Katrina taught us many important lessons. Unlike other hurricanes that blow quickly across the coastal plain and then dissipate, Katrina malingered and maintained her strong force into the central state area. She unleashed a force on landlocked cities in ways previously unfelt.

Following are some suggestions about how institutions can anticipate and respond to a crisis. They should help any campus maintain the integrity of its operations and people in the face of any anticipated crisis.

NEW DIRECTIONS FOR STUDENT SERVICES • DOI: 10.1002/ss

Create a detailed emergency management plan beforehand. The plan can help preserve the structural integrity of campus operations that would be endangered by the crisis. Future emergency response plans at Millsaps will include advance purchases of supplemental drinking water and gasoline. The absence of safe water was initially a mild surprise, but our alarm grew when the city announced that the water treatment processing center could not function. In addition, the loss of electricity confounded us because it included the inability to pump gasoline into our vehicles.

Adequate supplies are one outcome of good planning. They are important, and the process of planning might be more important to the integrity of the campus community before, during, and after a crisis. By adding the following elements, the plan becomes part of the consistent structure of the institution beforehand, involving all constituent groups. Otherwise, the plan is reactive instead of proactive, the property of situational leaders instead of the entire campus, and disconnected from normal operations. To be more effective, campuses must:

- Engage representatives from all areas of the college in the development of the plan, including students.
- Locate and commission campus emergency response experts to assess campus preparedness, if budgets permit.
- Practice actions required in the plan.
- Broadcast the plan via multiple methods.
- Publish the plan on the institution's web site.

Maintaining Leadership Integrity

Blanchard (2007) wrote that integrity was the number one characteristic that employees want in leaders. The community wants it too. They want to trust that you are doing all that you can on their behalf during a crisis. Just be prepared for them to second-guess how you performed after the crisis is over. To reassure them during and after the crisis:

Keep Calm.   During a period of turmoil, campus and community members turn to administrative leaders for guidance and hope, but the impact is overwhelming leaders because everyone is immersed in the same turmoil. Emotions are highly contagious, so leaders must remember the higher purposes of mission and responsibility, and rely on the practical aspects of thorough planning, in order to extend a calming hand that can calm panicked people.

Humor Helps.   In *The Integrity Crisis*, Rowland Croucher (2003) wrote: "If you want to learn what a person is really like, ask three questions: What makes him laugh? What makes him angry? What makes him weep?" Maintaining an appropriate, healthy, and thoughtful sense of humor helps keep community members, staff, and leaders calm during a crisis and afterward. Spontaneous humor is needed in the first phase of a crisis to

NEW DIRECTIONS FOR STUDENT SERVICES • DOI: 10.1002/ss

relieve tensions and overcome fear (Rodriguez, 2008). Immediately after the crisis, positive humor builds the survivors' sense of optimism. However, sarcastic and negative feelings emerge soon after, as survivors become bitter about their loss. Leaders need to maintain a realistic and nonjudgmental sense of humor during that time, to help the survivors rebuild their sense of community and common experience (Rodriguez, 2008).

As we regathered our thoughts about Hurricane Katrina for this chapter, we discovered that we would rather laugh and smile about the collective resolve, the boundless love, the affable new friendships, the extended handshakes, the tangible and intangible generosity, and the resecured protections at the heart of our stories.

Listen, Listen, Listen.   "None of us is as smart as all of us." This comment by Ken Blanchard, Don Carew, and Eunice Parisi–Carew (2000) is a key to institutional integrity in crisis. Everyone in and around Millsaps helped us plan for, react to, and recover from Hurricane Katrina. Listening to them was the key to gaining their assistance. We hope we were as attentive, caring, and interested in truly hearing other voices as we remember we were, but we do not forget how easily people could be agitated and aggressive. It was hard for anyone to hear through the swirling winds.

Communicate, Communicate, and Oh Yes, Communicate.   Accurate, timely, and ongoing information sharing is critical to maintain ethical and structural integrity on campus. Signage, individual visits to residence halls and fraternity houses, and other forms of traditional communication should be used to inform the community before, during, and after any crisis.

Consistency is an important aspect of integrity, and students, faculty, and staff must know where they can find material to use during any anticipated crisis. Consistency includes time as well as place, so regular meetings must be scheduled for at least two groups. First, the emergency management and response team must know when and where regular meetings will take place. When the leaders of the crisis response team are well informed, then they can raise questions and feel empowered to relay helpful and thorough information. Second, a town hall meeting must be scheduled for the constituents of the community during the crisis. It should be every day at the same time and place. At Millsaps, the entire community met in the cafeteria each day at 6 P.M.

Take Care of Yourself.   Numerous administrators slept in their offices, subsequently discovering that six hours in an office armchair is not restful, nor does it enhance good posture! Other setbacks—such as water shortages and the lack of electric power—eroded the strengths of leaders, too. Thus, steps must be taken to conserve one's energy and inspiration. Fifteen to thirty minutes of privacy, each day, can help leaders recenter their physical and psychological energies. Protecting this respite is an ethical obligation, and it helps individuals protect their physical, emotional, and spiritual wholeness.

NEW DIRECTIONS FOR STUDENT SERVICES • DOI: 10.1002/ss

Dealing With the Emotional Aftermath

Work began on this chapter five-and-a-half years after Katrina, yet the tragedy remains fresh and emotions still raw. People feel angry, afraid, shocked, sad, guilty, frustrated, and exhausted. Many are mentally as well as emotionally drained because they spent so much energy providing nonstop service to our students and their off-campus families during the crisis. "Survivors' guilt" was not uncommon among staff who avoided significant losses while so many students and their families lost their property and livelihoods.

The sheer magnitude of the losses overwhelmed God-fearing, law-abiding, innocent people. They felt spiritually abandoned, and no one rejoiced about the remnants of their lives that were left in the hurricane's wake. Yes, numerous churches and synagogues from all over the country reached into the horror zone. They helped diminish some of the spiritual void by listening and praying with the victims, but resentment was voiced against the power of Mother Nature, the wrath of God, and our inability to do much to thwart harm to so many kind people.

All these emotions are signs of posttraumatic stress disorder, which threatens to linger for years. New research studies show that many are as stressed today as they were weeks after the storm. Regrettably, the people who had the least before the storm were damaged the most. They could not afford or find access to the resources they needed to get help.

The Continuing Bureaucratic Nightmare

Residents were outraged at our national leadership's inability to respond to the storm. Federal Emergency Management Agency (FEMA) employees did not show up until weeks after the storm, and years later, housing and insurance issues are still unresolved for many. The shattered buildings at our sister institution, the University of Southern Mississippi—Gulf Park campus, are lingering echoes of the storm's wrath.

Institutions and individuals have spent years providing paperwork, over and over, to justify every detail of the same requests. The numbers of new forms are an ironic contrast to the numbers of old records that were lost in the storm. The value of property cannot be proven, yet the owners have to prove its worth to bureaucrats. Few community members can afford to rebuild anywhere near water, due to skyrocketing insurance prices. Fairness seems forever gone for many.

Final Reflections

Hurricane Katrina dissipated, but the destruction of property, the magnification of fear and worry, and the financial and emotional costs to families remain. Despite nature's irresistible power, the colleges caught in its path

NEW DIRECTIONS FOR STUDENT SERVICES • DOI: 10.1002/ss

learned much for the next encounter, hoping that similar gales are eons away. President Lucas said, "Katrina made us more aware than ever of the forces of nature, and that we are not in charge. I think that, spiritually, that can be a riveting realization. We just aren't as in charge of things as we think we are."

Things can be replaced. People are priceless. The heart of integrity and the epicenter of leadership is the obligation to care for the people we serve. Our focus on maintaining the campus community cannot waver, and time cannot stop it. John Lennon said, "Life is what happens to you while you're busy making other plans." We entered the fall of 2005 with many wonderful strategic goals and objectives for our community, but the hurricane pushed them aside. We cannot restore those particular plans, so we have replaced them. It is time to move the new plans forward. Integrity demands it.

References

Blanchard, K. *Heart of a Leader: Insights on the Art of Influence.* New York: David C. Cook, 2007.
Blanchard, K., Carew, D., and Parisi-Carew, E. *The One Minute Manager.* New York: Harper Collins, 2000.
Croucher, R. The Integrity Crisis, January 5, 2003. Retrieved February 22, 2011, from http://jmm.aaa.net.au/articles/9872.htm
Rodriguez, G. Laughter is the Best Medicine: Humor in Crisis Situations, January 21, 2008. Retrieved February 22, 2011, from www.associatedcontent.com/article/542321/laughter_is_the_best_medicine_humor.html?cat=68.

FRANCES LUCAS is the vice president and campus executive officer of the University of Southern Mississippi and president emerita of Millsaps College. BRIT KATZ is vice president of student affairs at Millsaps College.

INDEX

ACPA. *See* American College Personnel Association (ACRA)

ACPA Statement of Ethical Principles and Standards (ACPA), 71

Allen, K., 50–51

Alliance to Advance Ethics and Compliance Best Practices for Higher Education, 19

Alstete, J. W., 28, 29

Alverno College, Milwaukee, 60, 63

American Association of University Professors (AAUP), 19

American College Personnel Association (ACRA), 45, 70

American Council on Education (ACE), 8, 54–55

American Productivity and Quality Center, 60

American Red Cross, 91

Ancient Greeks, 6

Anderson, M. S., 21

Annual Higher Education Conferences (Society of Corporate Compliance and Ethics), 20

Antony, J. S., 20–21

Armino, J., 27, 30

Association of College and University Auditors, 19

Astin, A., 45, 46

Astin, H., 45, 46

Atwood, M., 10

Auburn University, 19

Austin, A. E., 21

Babson College, 50

Bad Leadership (Kellerman), 49

Badaracco, J., 1, 47, 48

Baird, L., 2, 7, 15, 16, 21, 22

Baldridge, J. V., 7

Banjamin, M., 69–71

Banta, T. W., 3, 5, 9, 18, 53, 58, 60

Barr, M., 9, 50, 51

Basken, P., 69

Bastido, M. N., 20

Baxter Magolda, M. B., 73

Becker, T., 1, 2

Beesmyer, L. A., 19–20

Benjamin, M., 69–71

Bennis,W., 3

Berea College, 16

Berger, J. B., 16, 18

Berry, W., 1

Bertram Gallant, T., 19–20

Bickel, R., 69

Black, K. E., 60

Blake, E., 9

Blanchard, K., 93, 94

Blimling, G. S., 72

Bok, D. C., 17, 69

Bolman, L., 6

Bousquet, M., 49

Bowyer, K., 61

Boyer, E., 10

Braxton, J. M., 16, 18, 21, 22

Briggs, L., 1

Brown, Douglas, 61, 62

Brown, M., 5

Brown, R. D., 56, 68

Bryan, W., 30

Butts, J. L., 3, 67

California, 46

Campbell, J., 86

Carducci, R., 47, 49

Carew, D., 94

Carnegie, A., 29

Carnegie Foundation for the Advancement of Teaching, 29

Carpenter, S., 30

Carter, S., 2, 6

CAS. *See* Council for the Advancement of Standards (CAS)

CAS Book of Standards, 31

CAS Characteristics of Individual Excellence for Professional Practice in Higher Education, 28

CAS General Standards, 28; Ethics (Exhibit 3.1), 32

CAS Statement of Shared Ethical Principles, 28

Center for Academic Integrity, 17

Center for College Affordability and Productivity, 29

Characteristics of Individual Excellence for Practices in Higher Education, 31

Cherrey, C., 50–51

Chickering, A., 54, 59

Chris (case), 27, 28, 31, 32

City University of New York (CUNY), 19

Clark, B. R., 21
Clement, L., 80–81, 85
Cohen, W., 2
Contreras-McGavin, M., 47, 49
Cooper, D., 68, 72, 74
Cooper, D. L., 68, 72, 74
Cornell University, 20
Corts, T., 60, 62, 63
Council for the Advancement of Standards in Higher Education(CAS), 2, 16, 27, 29, 30, 32; challenges for, 33; and elements of standards, 30–31; and focus on standards, 31; and individual excellence, 31–33; uses of, 30–33
Courage to Teach (Palmer), 69
Cox, D., 15
Creamer, D. G., 31, 33, 72
Croucher, R., 93

Dalton, J., 7
Dangerfield, R., 9
Dartmouth College, 19
Deal, T., 6
Dean, L. A., 68
Delgado Community College, 92
Dewey, J., 54–56
Dillard University, 92
Doherty, A., 60
Dore, T. M., 21
Durer, M., 62
Dyersburg State Community College (Tennessee), 61

Economic recession (2007-2010), 57
Effective Leadership in Student Services (Rickard and Clement), 80–81
"Eight Great Commitments" (Berea College), 16
Ellsworth, R., 1
Enron, 1
Estanek, S. M., 46
Ethical integrity, 6–7; and compromising realities, 10; and contractual caring, 10–11; and contractual conformity, 11; and ethical ideals, 10; and relating virtues of integrity to different types of institutions, 6–7; and student affairs, 9–11; virtues of, 6
Ethics Point, 19
Etzkowitz, H., 17
Evans, N., 7

Facebook, 68
Family Educational Rights and Privacy Act (FERPA), 42–43
Federal Emergency Management Agency (FEMA), 95
Fletcher, J., 46
Florida, 19
Frameworks, for teaching integrity: and ethical standards and principles, 70; external, 69–70; and moral virtues, 70–71
Fried, J., 16, 70–71

Gamson, Z., 59
Garvin, L., 90
Georgia Tech, 62
Germany, 31
Gochenauer, P., 30
Golde, C. M., 21
Gonyea, R. M., 59
Guidelines, 31
Gulf of Mexico, 89
Guthrie, V. L., 73

Halx, M. D., 72–73
Hamrick, F. A., 69–71
Harper, D., 31
Harris, N. F., 20
Harrison, L. M., 2, 45, 47
Hartman, L., 5
Healey, P., 17
Healy, M., 7
Henkel, M., 21
Hero with a Thousand Faces (Campbell), 86–87
Hirschy, A. S., 16, 18
Hirt, J. B., 72, 75
Hurricane Katrina, 3; continuing bureaucratic nightmare of, 95; dealing with emotional aftermath of, 95; final reflections on, 95–96; integrity and, 89–96; and local community, 91; and maintaining institutional integrity, 92–93; and maintaining leadership integrity, 93–94; and restoring campus community, 92; and serving displaced students, 92
Hutchings, P., 60

Illinois, 19
Inevitability, 80
Integrity: challenges to, 17–18; creating culture of, 19–20; enhancing, in student affairs, 18–19; healing power of,

85–86; and Hurricane Katrina, 89–96; and ideal description based on best practice, 16–17; integrating, into graduate training, 20–23; philosophical description of, 15–16; promoting, through standards of practice, 27–34; specific ways CAS standards address, 30–33; and student affairs leadership, 80–81; in student affairs organizations, 15–23; in teaching, 67–75

Integrity, professional challenges to, 79–87; and cultural identification, 82; and faith, 85; generating hypotheses about, 86; and healing power of integrity, 85–86; and identification challenges, 81–82; and identification with prior administrations, 82; and inevitability, 80; and institutional conflicts, 82–83; and loyalty conflicts, 82–85; and loyalty to prior administration, 84; and loyalty to staff, 84; and loyalty to students, 84–85; and personal identification, 82; and reputations and resources, 83–84; and student affairs leadership, 80–81; types of, 81

Integrity, teaching, 67–75; and activating reflection, 71; beginning with frameworks in, 69–71; and current contexts that make integrity important to learn, 68–69; and individual beliefs, 71; methods for, 73–75; and teaching locations, 72–73; teaching philosophies in, 73; teaching relationships in, 75

Integrity Crisis (Croucher), 92

Iowa University, 19

Jackson, Mississippi, 89, 90

James Madison University (Virginia), 61, 63

Jimenez, A. L., 72–73

Johnson, D. W., 74

Johnson, F. P., 74

Jones, E. A., 60

Katz, R. B., 3, 89

Keating, L., 50, 51

Keeling, R. P., 64

Kelderman, E., 29

Kellerman, B., 49

Kerr, C., 51

Kezar, A., 19–20, 47, 49

Kidder, R. M., 3, 68, 80

Kinzie, J., 59–60

Kirp, D., 50

Kitchener, K., 70

Knefelkamp, L. L., 56

Kolb, D. A., 73

Komives, S., 2, 9

Komives, S. R., 27

Kouzes, J., 46

Ku Klux Klan, 82

Kuh, G. D., 35, 59, 60

LaCaze, M., 15

Lake, P., 69

Lazerson, E., 61

Leading with Soul (Bolman and Deal), 6

Lefebvre, L. A., 60

Lennon, J., 96

Leslie, L. L., 17

Levine, M., 15

Lewis, H., 49–50

LGBT (lesbian, gay, bisexual, and transgender) students, 18

LGBT Center, 27, 28, 31

Lipka, S., 68

Lloyd, J., 68

Lloyd-Jones, E. M., 54–56

Lohmann, J., 62

Love, P., 9, 33, 46

Lowney, C., 46

Lucas, F., 3, 79, 89, 96

Lyons, J., 35

Mable, P., 29

Machiavelli, N., 47

Macintyre, A., 1, 5–6, 11

Malmberg, M., 62

McCaffrey, S. A., 70

McClain, C., 61

McClendon, S. A., 16, 18

McCloskey, D., 10

McKeachie, W. J., 74

Merriam-Webster.com, 27

Meyerson, D., 48

Middle States Association (MSA), 1

Miller, T. E., 2, 9, 35, 43

Miller, T. K., 30, 56

Miller, W., 61–62

Millsaps College, 3, 89–94; campus community, 90–91; maintaining institutional integrity at, 92–93; restoring campus community of, 92

Minnesota, 19

Mississippi, 89

Mississippi Coliseum, 91

Mississippi Delta region, 90

MSA. *See* Middle States Association (MSA)
Mt. Hood Community College (Oregon), 62
Mullendore, R., 30
Music Man (musical), 82
Musschenga, A., 6

Narvaez, D., 73
Nash, R., 22–23, 70
NASPA. *See* National Association of Student Personnel Administrators (NASPA)
National Association of College and University Business Officers (NACUBO), 19
National Association of Student Personnel Administrators (NASPA), 19, 45, 70; Mid-level Professionals Institute, 50
National Collegiate Athletic Association (NCAA), 19, 83
National Oceanic and Aeronautical Administration, 89
New Orleans, Louisiana, 90
Northeast Missouri State University, 61
Northouse, P., 46

Organizational integrity: and ethical integrity, 6–7; and structural integrity, 5–6; of student affairs, 7–8; suggestions for practice of, 11–12; virtues of, 5–13

Packham, D., 22
Paine, L., 2, 6, 36
Palmer, P. J., 69, 73
Parisi-Carew, E., 94
Parker, C. A., 56
Parks, S. D., 47
Paterson, B., 30
Paulson, K., 60
Penney, J., 9
Posner, B., 46
Priest, D. M., 17
Prince, J. S., 56
Progressive Education Movement (1920's), 54

Queer Student Coalition, 84–85

Reason, R., 7
Rest, J. R., 73
Reybold, L. E., 72–73

Rhoades, G., 17, 22
Rickard, S., 80–81, 85
Rip, A., 21
Roberts, D. C., 3, 5, 18, 53, 54
Rodriguez, D. P., 59
Rodriguez, G., 93–94

Saint Paul, 6
Samford University (Alabama), 60, 63
Sandeen, A., 9
Sanford, N., 12, 54
Sarbanes-Oxley Act, 19
Saunders, S. A., 3, 67, 69, 70, 72, 74
Schot, J. W., 21
Schroeder, C., 9, 61, 63
Schuh, J. H., 30, 59–60
Sinclair, A., 46
Slaughter, S., 17, 22
Smith, M. R., 55, 56
Society of Corporate Compliance and Ethics, 20
Sork, T., 22
Southern Illinois University, Edwardsville, 61
Spier, R. E., 21–22
Sporn, B., 17
St. John, E. P., 17
Standard, 31
Standards: history of, in student affairs, 29–30; of practice, promoting integrity through, 27–34; role of, in professional practice, 28; and self-regulation, 28
Statement of Ethical Principles and Standards (ACPA), 16
Strange, C., 54
Structural integrity, 5–6; and empirical consistency and coherence, 8–9; of student affairs, 8–11
"Student Affairs as Change Agents" (NASPA Mid-level Professional Institute; Barr and Keating), 50
Student affairs leadership, integrity and, 80–81
Student Development, integrity in: and assessment as example of theory and practice, 58–63; concluding reflections on, and assessment, 63–64; defining terms in, 54; emergence of attention to, 54–58; and implementation, 61–62; and improvement, 62–63; and linking ideal of theory with practice, 58; and planning, 60–61

Student Development: How to Make the Most of College Life (Walters), 55
Student Personnel Point of View (American Council on Education), 8–9, 16, 53–55
Suggs, W., 69

Tasker, M., 22
Taylor, E., 20–21
Teaching integrity. *See* Integrity, teaching
Tempered radical, 48
Terkel, S., 10
Texas A&M University, 19
Thomas, R., 3
Thomas, W., 9, 81
Tierney, W. G., 17
"Tomorrow's Higher Education" project, 56
Transactional leadership: and accessibility, 39–41; and adaptability to individual interests and needs, 41; and assessment possibilities, 43; clarity and consistency in, 37–38; and confidentiality, 42; and fairness and openness in funding and fees, 38; framework and guiding principles for, 36–37; and full disclosure, 39; and honesty and accuracy, 42; integrity in, 35–44; and limited resources, 35–36; and problem solving, 42–43; and simplicity, 38–39; and staff responsiveness, 41; and student as partner, 41–42
Transformational (term), 45
Transformational leadership: and acknowledging realities of leadership, 47–48; dichotomy, 45–46; power problem in, 46–47; and reinserting power analysis into student affairs' leadership discourse, 50–51; and strategies for creating more transformational systems, 48–50
Trevino, L., 5

Trow, J. A., 35
Truman State University, 61, 63
Tulane University, 92
Tull, A. T., 72
Twain, M., 85

United States Department of Education, 28
University of California, 20
University of Charleston (West Virginia), 62
University of Missouri, Columbia, 61, 63
University of Nevada, Las Vegas, 19
University of New Orleans, 92
University of Southern Mississippi, Gulf Park, 95
Upcraft, M., 7, 30
U.S. Naval Academy, 61–62

Vicksburg, Mississippi, 90–91
Voorhees, R. A., 60

Wade, P. P., 90
Walters, J. E., 55
Washburn, J., 49
Webster, A., 17
Webster's New World Dictionary, 54
Westhues, K., 10
Whitt, E. J., 59–60
Widick, C., 56
Williams, B., 15
Wingspread Seven Principles for Good Practice in Undergraduate Education, 59
Winston, R. B., 31, 69, 70, 72, 75
Woodard, D., 9
World War II, 55
Wulff, D. H., 21

Young, R. B., 1, 5, 7, 10, 16, 36, 37, 44, 79

Ziman, J. M., 21